A Country House:

John Calvin Stevens, Arch't:

TURN-OF-THE-CENTURY HOUSE DESIGNS

*With Floor Plans, Elevations and
Interior Details of 24 Residences*

William T. Comstock

DOVER PUBLICATIONS, INC.
New York

Bibliographical Note

This Dover edition, first published in 1994, is an unabridged republication of the work originally published by William T. Comstock, New York, in 1893 under the title *Suburban and Country Homes*.

Library of Congress Cataloging-in-Publication Data

Suburban and country homes.
  Turn-of-the-century house designs : with floor plans, elevations, and interior details of 24 residences / William T. Comstock.
      p.   cm.
  Originally published: Suburban and country homes. New York : W.T. Comstock, 1893.
  ISBN-13: 978-0-486-28186-5 (pbk.)
  ISBN-10: 0-486-28186-8 (pbk.)
  1. Suburban homes—United States—Designs and plans.   2. Eclecticism in architecture—
United States.   I. Comstock, William T.   II. Title.
NA7571.S84   1994
728'.37'0222—dc20   94–12113
                                                                                  CIP

Manufactured in the United States by Courier Corporation
28186806   2014
www.doverpublications.com

PREFACE.

THE object of this book is to present to intending builders and those interested in building a variety of designs for houses of moderate cost. The designs have been contributed by architects who have made a study of domestic architecture, and illustrate how a house reasonable in cost can, by the intelligent use of different materials, be just as artistic as one to which no limit of cost has been attached.

ARCHITECTS WHO HAVE CONTRIBUTED DESIGNS TO THIS BOOK.

John Calvin Stevens.....................................Portland, Me.
Charles P. Baldwin.......................Prudential Building, Newark, N. J.
William A. Lambert.......................114 Nassau Street, New York.
Yarnall & Goforth..............14 South Broad Street, Philadelphia, Pa.
E. G. W. Dietrich.............................18 Broadway, New York.
E. L. Messenger.................................Brooklyn, N. Y.
Manly N. Cutter..........................203 Broadway, New York.
Theo. Hopping...............28 South Willow Street, Montclair, N. J.
George Martin Huss....................1285 Broadway, New York.
Otto J. Gette.........................378 Sackett Street, Brooklyn, N. Y.
Frank W. Beall. ....318 Broadway, New York.
L. S. Buffington...............................Minneapolis, Minn.
Creighton Withers.........................21 State Street, New York.
A. W. Cobb.........................Winthrop Highlands, Mass.
A. L. C. Marsh..........................90 Nassau Street, New York.
McCurdy & Pulis..............................Denver, Col.
Stanley S. Covert...........................19 Park Place, New York.
John Brower, Jr.............109th Street and Riverside Drive, New York.
E. R. Tilton............................21 State Street, New York.

All inquiries regarding the designs in this book should be addressed to the architects, who will be pleased to furnish whatever information is necessary.

Suggestions on House Building.

By A. W. COBB, Architect.

IT IS my purpose in offering these suggestions to do so somewhat in the manner in which an architect would advise his client in the process of designing a house. It is intended to carry the reader through the various stages of progress, from the first rough sketches portraying the house as it will appear on the site selected, to its completion and delivery to its owner. Every house, when it seeks to fulfill its conditions as a dwelling and meet the personal requirements of any special family, is in so far a new invention; and the architect has for his problem not only the architectural questions involved, but the character of his client and his client's family to study, that he may build a house adapted to the habits of its future occupants; otherwise he goes wide of the mark in furnishing them with a home, however ornamental may be his design.

The client naturally desires the handsomest and most convenient house that the money appropriation will allow; this may safely be assumed at the outset.

We will also assume that we are discussing the building of houses of a suburban or rural character, such as are portrayed in the designs herewith presented. Let us trace, then, the processes by which the idea of the house to be built is expressed in drawings and specifications, and embodied in the actual building. And at the beginning let us measure rightly the value of this formulation and expression of the house idea, which is the chief function of the architect.

"Whatever a man makes is always a thought before it is a material thing. This is true of all things from a pin to an empire. * * * A steam engine is only a great idea dressed in iron, and it ran in somebody's head before it was set a-going on any railroad. * * * Michael Angelo, at Rome, when building Saint Peter's Church, had to work years long in setting up the structure in thought; myriad details of the great edifice had their patterns in Michael Angelo's mind before they became tangible things." And, as it was with great Saint Peter's, so it is in kind with the design and construction of even the simplest dwelling.

The architect's first definite step in the process of materializing the house idea is the making of study-plans and sketches. These sketches, made in various styles, pen and ink, pencil or color, usually give the client the first tangible expression of the appearance of his proposed house. The architect will at the outset endeavor to obtain in professional consultations the ideal of his client. This ideal structure will always have its "local coloring," under the influence of

individual tastes, or suggested by other houses. Here the architect's sketch plans and perspective are most important in putting into shape the house idea, which he and his client have been developing:

The sketches having proved satisfactory, the next step is the elaboration of working drawings; first the plans and elevations at "quarter scale"; then the masonry and framing drawings; details—many at full size—and the specifications; which calculated to guide the builder in constructing the house, which the original sketches have portrayed. By the time that these working drawings and specifications are ready for estimates, the location of the house on the lot has been settled, so that grade lines, outside steps, roadways and terraces can all be definitely shown, preventing any misunderstanding as to amount of excavating, face-underpinning, etc.

The lot has usually been secured before the architect is called in, although sometimes not only is his advice asked in the selection, but he is asked to develop the design as a help in deciding which one of two or more lots will be best adapted to the style of house which the client desires. The most desirable lot for an all-the-year house in our "temperate" clime, is evidently one on a slope somewhere between south-east and southwest, with a shelter of trees or sharp rise of ground to the north or west; the whole contour giving such trend of surface water as to insure a dry cellar. Our early colonial settlers, who had plenty of land to choose from, usually selected sites of this character for their dwellings. But in these present days, when a rapidly-increasing population is gathering around great centres and when land values are higher than they were in colonial days, the lot-hunter of moderate means, who wishes to locate within reach of his business, must take the best lot of land that offers for the money, even though it may not slope to the sun, and even if it requires a rubble drain, with a proper free outlet, to insure a dry cellar. But actual swampy land should be tabooed for residence purposes, unless it can be filled in to a proper grade.

Provided the lot chosen for the dwelling be wholesomely high and dry, the house may be successfully adapted to it, whatever be the slope of the land or its compass frontage to the street. The rooms may be so disposed as to invite the cheerful sunshine, and to repel the prevalent cold winds of the region. The most marked style of house accomplishing this purpose is the old-fashioned farm house, with its two or three stories to the sun, and its long lean-to or shed roof to the north. Various adaptations of this meritorious idea are successfully worked into many of our modern American houses.

As before stated, it is assumed that we are discussing the building of houses of a suburban or rural character. To be quite specific, we will assume the scene of house building to be the suburbs of some large city.

Before proceeding to discuss the details of finishing the house, as these will develop under the combined super-vision of the client and architect, let us consider further the question of site, the adaptability of the house to its surroundings. And this signifies not alone the mere planning of the house on its individual lot. To harmonize the house with its surroundings it is necessary to consider the aggregate of houses as a settlement, and their relations to each other. I wish to urge strongly here the necessity of taking this general view, because this matter is too often lost sight of. An injudicious building up of a once picturesque, sylvan neighborhood may in a few years transform it into a mere compacted, systemless aggregate of heterogeneous buildings. The very people who had been attracted to a place by its rural beauties may, by their heedless placing of houses, shops and stables, rob it of its charms. Ill-advised cutting of trees, blasting of beautiful moss-grown rocks, neglect in adopting uniform frontage lines and failure to reserve a choice tract here and there for public parks, and other like methods of procedure, may effectually blight what could have been developed into a beautiful settlement.

I have in mind a happy instance of the right method of

procedure in a certain suburb of St. Louis. At the beginning of its development land speculators had blocked out the whole territory into streets and building lots, and the process of covering it with an ill-considered settlement had begun. But control of the tract was later secured by parties who worked it over on a new plan. An area of several acres at the centre was set aside for a public park, avenues were run with regard to artistic effect, stringent rules as to front lines of buildings, location of stables, etc., were incorporated in the land deeds. The result is that the neighborhood which was once in a fair way to be marred is now a most delightful colony, grouped around its central park; every residence street a parkway in itself, with shade trees and ample lawn space.

I have devoted considerable space to this particular branch of the subject, because that while it is not usually dealt with in the specifications and other routine documents of the architect's office, it is yet as vitally important to the house-builder and house-owner as the question how he shall paint his house, or what shall be the style of his wall papers.

Having thus discussed the larger landscape relations of the house and the considerations which should prevail in the securing of the lot and the location of the house upon it, let us proceed with the development of the house itself in detail. The foundation or cellar wall of our model house should be built with an outside batter and should be able to stand alone, free of the bank, before the filling in against the wall is done with loose stone or gravel. If the soil is sandy, so that surface water filters down through it readily, there will be no need of a rubble drain to secure a dry cellar, but if the cellar be dug in hard pan or ledges, there should be a trench not less than a foot deep and filled with loose stone, as a footing for the cellar wall. Or there may be a drain pipe of agricultural tile all around the foot of the wall outside. In either case the drain should have an outlet independent of the plumbing drain, if possible. If it is led into the house drain there should be a trap at the junction.

The exposed underpinning will be brick or stone. If the main walls of the house are also brick or stone, it is well enough, where the appropriation is limited, to make the walls solid without a vaulted air space; and furr the walls inside with 2x3 studding, set one inch clear of the wall. This gives ample air space and secures against moisture from the masonry striking through to the plaster. In this furring, as in all interior studding, fire stopping should be attended to. All chimney flues should be lined, making them thicker than four inches of brickwork. The lining may be fire clay pipe, round or square, or it may be brick set up edgewise, making a six-inch wall.

If the main walls be of wood the frame should be well braced with long braces extending from floor to floor in each story. These are far superior to short braces for insuring rigidity under wind pressure. The braces should not be cut clear through the four-inch studding; they should be 2x4 flatwise, gained two inches into studding and nailed at crossing of each stud. A house so braced will never rock distressingly in high winds; it will stand firm.

Opinion is divided as to merits of back plastering. Stout rosin-sized sheathing paper on wood walls, between boards and the wall shingles or clapboards, is necessary.

Whether the house have masonry or wood walls, either shingles or slating are allowable for sloping roofs. Gutters, though so often made of wood, are far better of metal, either galvanized iron or copper, which can be run up well under shingles or slates, with never a leaky back-joint. The conductor should be of same metals, and in case there is sewerage should be led into the house drain with a trap at each connection. Stopping conductors at grade or leading them into blind cesspools, occasion much annoyance, though this must often be done.

This much for certain essential features of construction. Let us now proceed to consider features of general arrangement and artistic finish of the house.

In a general way it may be said that the model house

which we are building should be designed according to the following rules. There should be consideration of:

1. PRIVACY.—The possibility of seclusion in each apartment, especially the bed chambers, yet with ready direct accessibility to the halls from each apartment.

2. COMFORT AND CHEERFULNESS.—It being remembered that the chief element of cheerfulness in a house is the sunshine, which should be freely admitted; covered piazzas being so placed as not to exclude direct sunlight from the rooms.

3. CONVENIENCE.—The plan being arranged to save steps in housework; compactly arranged, with no long or tortuous passages between rooms.

4. DIRECT LIGHT AND AIR.—No borrowed light or air, no skylight wells or light shafts; no inside bathrooms or water closets. In a suburban house standing free there is no excuse for makeshifts of borrowed light and ventilation for any apartment.

5. ASPECT AND PROSPECT TO BE CONSIDERED.—Aspect being the relation of the windows to sun and prevailing winds, and prospect being the view from the windows. A respected English authority on the subject of house designing discourses on this subject thus: "All over England there are examples of a 'well-built house,' as the auctioneers say, situated on rising ground, well sheltered, and affording a view of so many miles of fine country, with hills of neighboring shires in the distance; but how many instances are there of a house whose plan is adapted none the less to make the most of the scenery in this way, but also to give to every part of the residence its most suitable relation to the weather and the daily course of the sun."

Further it is recommended that the dining room have an easterly exposure, insuring the cheer of the morning sun at breakfast time; that library and parlor have south and west exposures; that some large window or group of windows, perhaps on the staircase landing, command the north landscape, which, lighted by the sun from behind the spectator, affords a pleasing picture, grateful to the eye.

And here is advice as to ornament, from the same authority; advice given in that spirit of fresh, assertive dogmatism which has made the British Empire:

6. ORNAMENT.—"Moderation in this, as in all else, is the rule, but nothing less; no exuberance, but no poverty. For there may be even in simplicity an affectation as demonstrative as any other; and when the fastidiousness of excessive refinement takes refuge in a mental blank, it is but an artificial idiocy in taste. * * * * A gentleman's house ought to be not merely substantial, comfortable and well furnished, but fairly adorned. It ought to exhibit a reasonable amount of intellectual liberality, faithfully keeping on the side of simplicity and moderation, *and clinging to the grace of elegance as the beauty which shall last the longest*; but avoiding none the less that poverty of dress which is not self-denial, but inhospitality."

For statement of the quality which makes the much-sought "style that wears well," the words in italics cannot be excelled. Grace of elegance, not vain show of over-wrought adornment, must ever characterize the styles which shall endure in the popular favor.

Following this canon of simple elegance, the most modest cottage may be made beautiful; externally, by force of graceful proportion, which implies adaptability to its site, and by harmonious color treatment; and internally, by the same attention to harmony in the color treatment of rooms effectively grouped to give pretty vistas. There is everything in this management of vistas—glimpses from one room to another—so that in looking from parlor to dining room you see the sideboard and in the reverse view the parlor fireplace, or the curtained bay with broad window seat is seen; or, looking from parlor to hall, the picturesquely disposed staircase terminates the view. This is what is meant by effective grouping of rooms—disposing their features so as to make the most of them. Fail to properly arrange these groupings, and the pretty features of your house may be only half effective, while with the proper arrangement the interior will interest and charm at every turn.

As to the interior wood finish of the house, various kinds of hardwood are beautiful and will stand more wear and tear than soft pine and whitewood. So for artistic and also for practical reasons hardwood finish, though much the more expensive to buy in stock and to work up, is yet desirable. When a client informs you his children are such young terrors to bang woodwork that he intends to finish inside with brown ash, there is nothing else but to say that it is a most excellent idea to finish in brown ash. Yet in a house where moderate cost is desired pretty effects, similar to hardwood in color, may be got by judicious use of stains covered with shellac and varnish. Take whitewood finish, for example. A stain composed of raw linseed oil, spirits and a *very little* Indian red, will give whitewood a perfect natural cherry color; a little raw umber will give oak color; raw burnt umber added to the raw umber will give brown ash. Burnt sienna with Indian red will give mahogany; simple burnt umber produces black walnut color. These stains for whitewood must be mixed very light and thin, and will then produce beautiful effects, the grain of the wood showing through them. The frequent mistake in using stains is making them too thick and strong in color, daubing the wood with them and obliterating the grain. For white pine finish the stain may be a trifle stronger than for whitewood. A good finish for these stained soft woods is one coat white shellac, well rubbed with fine pumice or very fine sand paper, and then given one coat very best coach varnish. This treatment of the woodwork by a conscientious painter, with the very best materials, is all that is required. Any further coats of shellac or varnish would be superfluous.

Where there is money to spare for it there may be many coats of shellac and varnish, with careful rubbing, to secure a dull gloss effect; but this expensive process is not really essential to the happiness of the occupants of the house.

Lead and oil painting requires three coats to cover well. The first coat should have very little lead; it should be chiefly raw linseed oil, color and a very little drying and white lead. A priming coat of this character will take a good hold on the woodwork, striking in well. Knots and sap-streaks in the woodwork should be touched over with white shellac *after* the priming coat is applied. Hardwood floors may be treated with filling shellac and a water-proof varnish if a shiny effect is desired, or with filling and wax polish if a dull gloss is preferred. But be sure your hard-wood floors will require frequent treatment, whether they be kept a bright or a dull gloss. Since we must have them, our hardwood floors cost us abundant labor, yet less, per-haps, than is involved in sweeping of carpets,

In wall papering, especially if plain cartridge papers are used, make sure the widths are closely butt-jointed by the paper-hanger. Occasional vertical streaks of white plaster showing at the joints after the paper has dried are undesir-able. Be cautious against arsenical wall paper and arsenical prepared paste. The persistent use of arsenic in the house-hold arts is one of the most malevolent features of our pres-ent civilization, and should be stamped out by organized effort. Stipulate that the paper-hanger make his own flour paste in the good old-fashioned way.

As to ceiling treatment, there are various good methods. Often the ceiling will look well in natural plaster. Elaborate stucco cornices and centre pieces are dispensable luxuries. A plain curved coving to take a frieze paper is a graceful treatment, with picture moulding at bottom of frieze and light bead on the ceiling. A pretty paneled ceiling may be cheaply made by light cross-mouldings nailed to furrings on the plaster. To make a timbered ceiling cheaply plane the joists and lay the lower floor of the room above of selected planed, matched and beaded sheathing, finished side down, running a light moulding around each panel of the ceiling. Papering plaster ceilings, or tinting them, with a few border lines of color or gilt, will produce pleasing effects.

Putting up chandeliers and brackets is a department of the finishing often superintended by the client. The method for gas chandeliers is obvious: they are screwed on the threaded ends of the outlets. For electric chandeliers use the crow's-feet screwed into the ceiling furrings. The long bolts running through the ceiling and fastened by a nut countersunk in the floor above are a needless expense and trouble in case of ordinary chandelier work.

Of house-heating it may be said in a general way that some system which provides an incoming current of fresh, warm air is the only right system. If direct radiators either steam or hot water, are used, there should be small wall openings to the outer air, with register for regulating the supply, behind some radiators. Good systems for supplying warmed fresh air, either by furnace or by indirect radiation, are abundant. A few fireplaces furnish the best of air outlets, taking the contaminated air from the lower part of the room. The bathroom, kitchen and laundry may well have ventilating registers.

The subject of plumbing will be thoroughly discussed elsewhere in the book. It is enough here to say that the most open, uncomplicated style of plumbing is the best.

Thus I have presented some of the details, large and small, to be considered in house-designing and building, from the time the architect is called in to the time when the family can say, "We are at home to our friends in our new house." This house-building, this providing the home-scene for human action, is a most worthy, an exalted work; and nothing will better carry client and architect happily through its often trying details, than will an appreciation of the sacred import of their task.

How to Plumb a Suburban House

Safely, Economically and Effectively, together with Plans and Specifications which may, with slight modification, be adapted to almost any Suburban Dwelling costing from $4,000 to $8,000.

By LEONARD D. HOSFORD.

The Disposal of Sewage.

There are in use some three practical methods of sewage disposal adapted to the average country residence where no public sewers exist. None of these three systems are perfect; in fact, none have proven entirely satisfactory, when, after a lapse of years, a minute investigation of their operations has taken place. The adaptation of any of these systems is limited somewhat to conditions, much depending upon the character of the surrounding soil, and, at times, upon the elevation of the premises, so that no one system can be specified to meet all conditions.

The first system, if system it may be called, and one which is largely in use to-day all over this country, is to dig a big hole in the earth, wall it up like a well with stone laid loosely, the top arched over and sodded, and into this the house drainage is carried, relying upon a porous soil to absorb the liquids, while the solids lodging in the shelving rock interstices are broken up and ultimately soak away into the ground, "out of sight, out of mind." If a cesspool of this character can be located from 200 to 500 feet away from any residence, if no danger of contaminating a water supply exists, and the cesspool top is below the level of the cellar bottom of the residence, and the character of the soil is loose, it may perhaps do no damage, and answer the purpose for several years before it finally chokes up, and the drain leading to it becomes full of solids. Then it is time, if not before, to dig a new cesspool.

A slight improvement on the single cesspool is the double cesspool system, the first of these being below ground, walled up and cemented water tight, the second excavated and walled up with stone loosely laid ; the house drain is then carried into the first at a point near the top, while an overflow is provided from the first to the second, this overflow pipe being carried down into the first cesspool to a point near the bottom, thereby forming a dam, which prevents most of the solids entering the second cesspool, but allows the liquids to overflow freely and soak away into the soil surrounding the second cesspool. This is sometimes called the twin cesspool system, and is much better than the single cesspool ; the solids being retained, the man-hole cover can be removed and the foecal matter excavated and sent to the compost heap. The adaptation of this manner of cesspool also requires a loose, dry soil or one that is underdrained, yet a great danger exists of water-supply contamination.

The second system which may be considered is that of Surface Irrigation, and can only be adopted when there is a large area of ground of character and location favorable. The space used for the reception of this system should be from one-eighth acre to one acre, and located from two to five hundred feet distant from any residence, and from ten to fifteen feet lower than the foundations of the premises discharging upon it. It consists, first, of a water-tight storage tank made of brick, wrought or cast iron, or perchance stone, and of capacity sufficient to store the entire waste disposal for a day, figuring on a fifty gallon per day per capita consumption. This storage tank may be situated near the house, with closed and sealed top, the drain pipe conducted into it, and once a day emptied by a lever-handled gate valve which can be pulled wide open. The discharge pipe connecting with this gate valve terminates at the drain- age field, which should be slightly sloping. At the point where this pipe discharges it is carried along the upper side of the drainage field with small branch outlets taken from the discharge pipe in such a manner as to distribute the sewage over a large area, which territory may be under cul- tivation as a special garden spot. Almost a complete dis- integration of the solids takes place in transit, and the distribution taking place daily before decomposition occurs to any great extent, there is no appreciable offense to the nostril or eye. The writer has used this system with con- siderable success in the plumbing of country residences. With this system there is little or no danger of the contami- nation of a water vein which may act as water supply to surrounding territory, as the rapid evaporation which en- sues on exposure to the sun, together with the oxidation of the gases produced by contact with the atmosphere, renders them comparatively harmless. Loose loam or sandy soil is a favorable condition in all of the systems under consideration.

The third system entitled to consideration as adapted to a country residence is called Sub-Surface Irrigation, the name in a measure explaining its function. It consists of a method of distributing the sewage by intermittent discharge of a flush tank through a system of pipes laid just under the surface of ground, i. e., from 8 to 12 inches, through a series of perforated pipes, or pipes laid in a disjointed man- ner, with from three-eighths to one inch of space between each length of pipe, and said space covered by loose collars of same radius as pipe. These pipes are spread out like a fan underneath the ground, laid from five to ten feet apart and substantially level, and are fed from a common pipe coming from the flush tank, which is arranged to discharge auto- matically or by the opening of a valve. When the discharge occurs this sub-system of piping is theoretically filled with sewage, which finds its way through the fissures before mentioned. The toilet paper and grease in the household wastes are serious detriments to this system, clogging the pipe interstices, and in many instances after a few years' use the entire system of drain pipes has to be dug up, cleaned and relaid. This system was used in many parts of England and the European continent for a number of years past by Mr. Roger Field, and was introduced in America by Mr. Geo. E. Waring, and is called here the Field-Waring system. This system is not patented, and is open to all who wish to employ it, although many of the devices adapted to the flush tank are patented.

In addition to the above it should be mentioned that a system of Sewage Filtration was experimented on by Mr. Scott West, a New York architect, and while his system was adapted to cities on a large scale, and is in use at pres- ent in some large Southern towns, he has never been suc- cessful in adapting a system of filtration to the wants of the suburban resident on a small scale. Chemical precipita- tion is too expensive and requires too much attention for the suburban resident to bother with.

After a brief consideration, therefore, of the methods of sewage disposal, providing there are no public sewers, it must resolve itself into a consideration of—

1. The single or the twin cesspool.
2. Surface irrigation.
3. Sub-surface irrigation.

A decision cannot be made as to the one best adapted without a knowledge of the conditions governing the case; therefore, assuming that the best adapted system will be ap- proved for the sewage disposal of the particular house in question after a thorough consideration of relative merits, let us proceed with the plumbing of the residence and the further problems of selecting materials therefor.

Soil Pipe.

Earthen pipe has been found to be the most durable pipe that can be employed for drainage when under ground and outside the house limits. We will therefore adopt earthen pipe, hard baked and salt glazed, to lead from our flush tank or cesspool to a point five or ten feet from the foundation walls of our house. Here we will discontinue its use, as earthen pipe is too fragile to be trusted inside the house limits, and we also require there a more perfect joint than one of cement, which is the only kind adapted to earthen pipe. Next comes the question of cast or wrought iron soil pipe.

Cast Iron Pipe for Drainage Purposes.

This pipe has been used for twenty years or more almost universally and with almost perfect success, the only objection being that there is an occasional sand hole in a casting, which, however, is always discovered when a pressure test is employed. The commercial standard is known as "extra heavy," and no other should be used. One more objection to cast iron pipe is urged by some, claiming that the necessary lead-caulked joints are not scientifically made, and that they are liable to be blown loose when the hubs are expanded by heat from escaping steam, which, sometimes happens, more especially in our city buildings. These two points, then, are made against cast iron pipe, viz., sand holes and liability to leakage caused by expansion of lead-caulked joints subjected to steam. In our particular country house we propose to test the cast iron soil and drain pipe to see if there are any sand holes, or perhaps pay the manufacturer an additional percentage to test it before he delivers it, and then we will plug up all the outlets and look for other leaks; so that this can hardly be an objection in our particular case. As for steam, there will be none connected with the drainage of our house.

Wrought Iron Pipe for Drainage Purposes.

Wrought iron pipe has been used to quite an extent within the past ten years with fairly satisfactory results. It is conceded, however, that wrought iron rusts away much more rapidly than cast iron for equal thickness of metal. This fact is easily demonstrated by placing a small section each of cast and wrought iron pipe in some moist place for a period of a few weeks.

Again, the screw thread joint which is cut on the pipe end deprives the piping at this point of about one-half its thickness. It is in this location that trouble may be looked for in connection with rapid oxidation.

The expense of erecting wrought iron pipe as soil and waste piping is somewhat greater than that of cast iron.

Recently it has been considered necessary when employing wrought iron for this purpose to thoroughly coat the piping with bitumen, coal tar or lead paint, which will for a time and to a certain degree resist oxidation. Just how long these coatings will last on the inside of the piping, when subjected to the gases and acids arising from waste disposal, is largely a matter of conjecture. Some theorists claim that when wrought iron pipe is employed for this purpose it should be zinc coated, or what is commercially termed galvanized.

As adapted to our particular house there seems to be, then, some objection to wrought iron in addition to the slight increase in expense, while with cast iron there is apparently no valid objection. A decision resulting from the consideration of the merits of these two particular substances, it may be argued, is, perhaps, only an opinion of the writer, yet personal experience leads me to believe that this opinion is based on sound principle.

In order to arrive at some conclusion, therefore, and after considering the above situation, it would seem that we might safely adopt cast iron pipe, in this instance at least.

Water Piping.

Next in order in the plumbing of our house we must consider the character of material to be employed for the water piping. Here also are three kinds of pipe in current use, viz.: lead, galvanized iron and brass. Lead pipe has been in use for hundreds of years for this purpose, giving excellent results, being reasonable in price and easily manipulated or repaired. In modern plumbing work, however, it has been found wanting in many points of adaptability of position, more particularly from point of appearance; also it is frequently necessary to suspend piping overhead, pendant from ceilings, which can hardly be done in a neat and effective manner except by continuous support when using lead. It, however, resists corrosion almost absolutely, except under special conditions. For underground water piping, in sand or loam, it is perhaps the best material which can be employed. We will, therefore, at least adopt it for our water service pipe to a point just within foundation wall, and for various other positions specified later in immediate connection with the plumbing fixtures proper, where it is necessary to employ a pipe easy of manipulation and adjustment. Galvanized wrought iron pipe forms an excellent water conductor, more especially for cold water; is about one-half the price of lead per lineal foot, can be neatly and quickly erected and is durable under ordinary circumstances with soft water. We will, therefore, consider favorably this piping for cold water supply purposes inside the house limits. It is not entirely satisfactory, however, when used for hot water, as the galvanized coating seems to peel off in scales on the inside, due perhaps to expansion, and the severe effect of boiling water on the bare iron pipe soon produces very rusty water. Clear water can be drawn, however, by allowing the faucet to remain open a few moments; yet it may prove a serious objection, as the fine linen from the laundry will frequently testify, an occasional rust spot on laundered wearing apparel presenting a most unsightly appearance. Brass pipe, tinned inside and out, is probably

as near a perfect article for hot water supply pipe as can be produced, and, although somewhat expensive—usually about twice the price per lineal foot of lead pipe (depending on the market)—it is well worth the additional cost from the results obtained. It should always be annealed, which renders it soft and ductile. It presents a fine appearance. and insures a clear water supply. On more expensive work it is customary to use this pipe entirely for both hot and cold water supply. With our particular house, however, where economy is an object, we will use it only on hot and circulation pipes—the circulation being part of the hot water system.

Plumbing Fixtures.

It is impossible at this time in the limited space provided to discuss exhaustively the relative merits of the large variety of plumbing fixtures. The following specifications will give the opinion of the writer as to what should be employed in the various capacities. These opinions will be undoubtedly subject to some criticism. The results obtained, however, are actual, and if the fixtures specified are employed in this or any other similar house, I am positive from experience the results will prove satisfactory.

The reader will note, should he be familiar with plumbing plans, that the piping section as well as the plumbing specification is at variance in many details with the principle adopted by health departments of various cities, as well as that of New York City; the difference being principally in the system or method of vent piping. In the adoption of any code of rules some standard has to be laid down, and a demand made that work conform in principle to the standard—hence the principle of "venting" each trap attached to the waste piping of a fixture which is imperatively demanded and adhered to religiously in plumbing work of nearly all large cities of to-day. There are positions, however, where the individual trap vent is superfluous; actually no occasion for it whatever. To discriminate on this point requires a thorough comprehension of the natural laws governing the case in hand.

The positions where the trap vent may safely be omitted are shown in part in the plumbing section. Where a fixture is near the main line of soil or waste pipe, so that the branch waste pipe is not more than two or three feet long, there is no good reason why a trap should be separately vented, provided the trap is so constructed that the discharge of an adjoining fixture will not siphon or cause an impairment of water seal. There are several traps made that will withstand such siphonic action, more notably the "Sanitas" and the "Delehanty."

The two objects attained by trap venting or back venting, as it

is termed in the plumbing trade, are: First, the preservation of the water seal in the trap when siphonic action is developed by the discharge of some adjoining fixture. Second, to assist in the aeration of the internal branch pipe leading to the trap of the fixture; the vent pipe "theoretically" producing a circulation of air within and over the branch system of waste piping, which is desirable; practically, however, this circulation of air in many instances amounts to little.

When the main lines of soil and waste piping are carried through the roof full size and the plumbing fixtures are situated immediately near those lines, so that the branches are not more than three to five feet long, and a trap is used that can not be siphoned under the conditions it is subjected to when in position, there is little or no need of wasting money on long lines of "back vent" pipes.

On the plumbing section it will be observed that I have shown and also call in the specification for the venting of the traps of the bath and basin, the only fixtures in the house which are trap vented. The following will explain why this is done: When the non-siphoning traps before mentioned are subjected in practice to strong siphonic action it produces in the trap an oscillation of the water caused by partial vacuum, which raises a continued gurgling sound lasting during the period of discharge of an adjoining fixture, and although the sound does no harm, still, to my mind, it is quite objectionable in or near a sleeping apartment—particularly as this same sound occurs in the ordinary S trap when it is being siphoned.

The plumbing of this residence can be done for $800, in accordance with plans and specification.

SEPARATE ESTIMATES.

Marble wainscot, as called for, put up at $1.25 per square foot.
Slate   "   "   "   75 cents per square foot.
Tiling in bathroom, "   "   75 to 85 cents per square foot.
Soapstone plastering, as called for, put up at 6 to 8 cents per square foot.

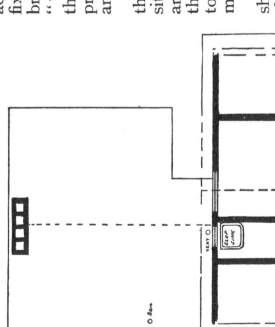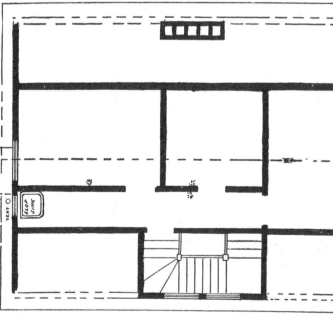

PLAN OF ATTIC.

Assuming that the sewer and water connections have been brought to a point ten feet from building line and that water pressure is from fifteen to sixty pounds per square inch, we will now write a specification for the plumbing, as shown on plans and section, Plates I. and II. and plan on Page 19.

SPECIFICATION FOR THE PLUMBING IN THE RESIDENCE OF MR. JOHN J. SMITH, ORANGE, N. J.

THOMAS JOHNSON, ARCHITECT, BROADWAY, N. Y.

House Drain.

The contractor will connect with the existing earthen drain pipe at point indicated on plan, about ten feet from the house line, and carry 4-inch extra heavy cast iron pipe to inside face of cellar wall, at which point insert a 4-inch house trap, with brass screw cover.

Fresh Air Inlet.

Provide a fresh air inlet of 4-inch extra heavy cast iron pipe and connect with house drain on inner side of "house trap" and extend same to a point 2 feet above grade and 15 feet from house line, terminating with a caged strainer, or vent cap, securely adjusted.

Soil Pipe.

Continue from house trap the 4-inch extra heavy cast iron drain pipe, as shown on plans, to a point 5 feet above the roof, leaving Y outlets at the cellar ceiling as follows: 4-inch to receive servants' closet, 2-inch for laundry tubs, kitchen sink, and vertical line of waste pipe from butler's pantry and slop sink; also 4-inch Y outlet for second story closet and separate 2-inch Y outlet for bath and basin, and 2-inch inverted Y outlet to receive the trap vent pipes of bath and basin.

Vertical Line of Waste Pipe.

Carry up from cellar ceiling a line of 2-inch extra heavy cast iron pipe to a point 5 feet above roof line, leaving 2-inch Y outlets, as shown, to receive the waste of pantry and slop sinks, increasing the vertical line of waste pipe to 4 inches at a point just beneath the roof line.

Joints in Iron Pipe.

All joints in iron pipe to be caulked with pig lead and oakum.

Cold Water Supply (Galvanized Iron).

Connect with the existing water service at a point about 10 feet from house line, a section of ¾-inch AA lead pipe, and continue to inside of cellar wall, passing through a 2-inch sheathing tube placed in foundation wall; provide a ¾-inch brass gate valve at this point. Provide just beyond this gate valve a ¾-inch outlet, which may hereafter be used for a sill or emptying cock, to which point the whole system of cold water will be graded. Leave the following outlets on the cold water supply pipe at cellar ceiling, each to be ¾-inch: For boiler, kitchen sink, laundry tubs, pantry sink, servants' closet, second story bathroom and slop sink line. Carry up one line of ¾-inch galvanized pipe to second story bathroom and one line of ¾-inch to pantry sink, with a ¾-inch stop valve at the foot of each line; the entire cold water piping of house to be ¾-inch galvanized iron from front wall.

Hot Water Supply (Tinned Brass).

Carry up from kitchen boiler to ceiling a line of ¾-inch tinned brass pipe and leave the following ¾-inch outlets on the kitchen ceiling, one each for tubs, sink and second story bathroom, and ½-inch each for pantry sink and third story slop sink; the second and third story lines to be controlled with gate valves at kitchen ceiling, all fittings to be tinned brass. All hot water piping to be tinned brass except as hereafter specified for short branches.

Circulation Pipe (Tinned Brass).

Carry up from bottom of boiler a line of ½-inch tinned brass pipe to second story (crossing kitchen ceiling) and connect in bathroom with the hot water pipe—placing stop valve at the foot of the line—all fittings to be tinned brass; lay pipe on slight return grade to bottom of boiler.

FIXTURES.

Servants' Closet.

Provide and erect one all-earthen siphon jet closet, as approved and selected by the architect and owner, with eight-gallon copper-lined cistern, chain pull and 1¼-inch rough brass flush pipe, 1¼-inch ash bracket seat (the above apparatus not to exceed list price of $40.00). Provide for closet apartment a 1¼-inch slate countersunk floor slab set flush with finished floor, same to be bedded in cement; size of slab to be 2 feet 6 inches deep by width of apartment, and have an 8-inch by ⅞-inch slate base on three sides. Connect closet to soil pipe, using short section of 4-inch "D" lead waste, brass floor flange and brass ferrule.

Laundry Tubs.

Provide and erect one set of two Yorkshire laundry tubs on bronzed iron pedestals, with brass plug, waste chain and stoppers; tubs to have rolled rims, with slate capping at back 5 inches wide; to be supplied with hot and cold water through ¾-inch brass and galvanized iron pipe and ¾-inch long "Fuller" cocks placed over top of tubs. Tubs to waste through 1½-inch "D" lead waste and 1½-inch "Sanitas" or "Delehanty" traps to the iron soil pipe and be connected therewith by brass ferrules; one trap for each tub.

Kitchen Sink.

Erect in kitchen one 18x36-inch rolled rim earthen Yorkshire kitchen sink standing at least three inches clear of wall all around; sink to be supported on three bronzed iron legs and supplied with hot and cold water through ¾-inch Fuller long shank cocks from ¾-inch brass and galvanized pipe. Sink to waste through 2-inch "D" lead waste to a Tucker grease trap, placed on floor at end of sink, arranged so as to be easy of access. Trap to waste through 2-inch "D" lead to 2-inch iron waste pipe, suspended on cellar ceiling; connect chilling chamber of grease trap with ¾-inch cold water pipe. Leave brass screw clean outs at all angles.

Boiler.

Provide and erect in kitchen one forty-gallon heavy pressure copper boiler, made from 2-pound copper, properly tinned and braced inside. Furnish bronzed iron boiler stand for same. Fit boiler up with ¾-inch brass pipe for hot water and ¾-inch galvanized pipe for cold water; the return from water back to be 1-inch brass pipe, with water back tapped full size. Provide stop valve on supply to boiler and ¾-inch emptying cock.

Pantry Sink.

Provide and erect in pantry one 16x28x6-inch flat-bottomed copper pantry sink, 20-ounce, with 2-inch recessed standing waste, and with 1½-inch Tennessee marble drain board, dished to sink; same to have 15-inch base on three sides of ⅞-inch Tennessee marble. Support slab by a 6-inch apron of 1-inch marble and support sink by a plaster of paris boxing supported on brackets or brass legs. Provide nickel-plated Fuller pantry cocks and supply with hot and cold water through ½-inch brass and ¾-inch galvanized pipe. Waste sink through 2-inch "D" lead waste to Tucker grease trap, standing on floor at side of sink; connect grease trap to 2-inch iron waste pipe, with short section of 2-inch "D" lead and 2-inch brass ferrule. Provide cold water connection to chilling chamber of grease trap.

Second Story Closet.

Erect in second story bathroom one siphon jet closet of same character as basement closet, the cistern to be of 1-inch whitewood, lined with 12-ounce copper and with rounded corners, to finish in white enamel paint and to rest on nickel-plated brackets. Furnish nickel-plated flush pipe and 1¼-inch oval ash or oak polished seat, with cover and nickel hinges; seat supported on nickel brackets. (The closet apparatus, as above 'specified, to be selected by architect and owner at a list price not exceeding $50.00.) Make the necessary waste connections, as before specified, and carry a ½-inch AA lead supply pipe to water closet cistern. Provide beneath closet an Italian marble floor slab, 3 feet wide by 2 feet 4 inches deep by 1¼ inches thick and bed same in cement flush with finished floor; place stop valves on hot and cold water pipes to control bathroom fixtures.

Basin.

Furnish and erect in same room one 36x24-inch countersunk Italian marble pier slab 1¼ inches thick, with 12-inch moulded back, same to be supported by two nickel-plated 1½-inch brass pipe legs, with dowel flanges top and bottom. Provide and adjust to slab a 15x19-inch white oval bowl, with 1½-inch nickel standing waste at back. Provide No. 3 large-nosed Fuller nickel basin cocks and ½-inch supply pipe of AA lead. Basin to waste through 1½-inch drawn lead vented S trap and 1½-inch "D" lead pipe ; vent pipe to be 1½-inch "D" lead. Provide floor slab 36x24 inches of 1¼-inch Italian marble and adjust as before. All supply and waste pipes to be above floor.

Bath Tub.

Furnish and erect one 5-foot 6-inch porcelain lined, rolled rim bath tub, with 1½-inch standing waste and with Fuller double supply cock, nickel plated; same to have hose and hand shower. Supply with water through ⅝-inch AA lead pipe and waste through 1½-inch "D" lead pipe and trap, as above; waste pipe to be increased to 2 inches at intersection of basin waste; vent pipe to be 1½-inch 'D" lead. No floor slab for this fixture.

Slop Sink.

Furnish and erect one rolled rim Yorkshire slop sink, size 16x22 inches, supported on 2-inch pedestal enameled iron trap; connect same to the 2-inch iron waste pipe by a short section of 2-inch "D" lead waste and 2-inch brass ferrule. Provide beneath same full width of apartment and 24 inches deep a 1¼-inch slate floor slab, set as before specified. Sheet walls, 4 feet high by 2 feet deep, with ⅞-inch slate, on all sides of sink. Provide ⅝-inch long Fuller supply cocks for hot and cold water.

Tests.

When all iron soil, waste and vent pipes are run and after all lead branches possible have been connected therewith, the ends will be sealed and the piping left filled with water until approved by architect or superintendent.

When a house is ready for occupancy and the entire plumbing is finished, the plumber will make a smoke test in presence of architect or superintendent.

HOW TO PLUMB A SUBURBAN HOUSE.

General Arrangement.

All soil, waste, vent and water piping will be permanently exposed to view. The vertical lines of soil and waste piping, where passing through important rooms, will be painted in white enamel or silver bronzed by the painter. The entire piping system to be supported clear of walls, on all sides, on neat galvanized pipe ring hangers, screwed to 1-inch moulded strips traversing the run of piping, neatly put up by the carpenter with screws.

Where it is absolutely necessary in any position to carry piping for short distance in a partition they shall be covered by a paneled board, hinged to frame, neatly cased and battoned, opening the entire length of enclosure.

The exterior of bath tub, closet cistern, slop sink standard, and the supply and waste pipes beneath the bath and basin, will be finished in white enamel or silver bronzed by the painter.

Submit Separate Estimate for this Work per Square Foot.

The architect or owner may provide, under another contract, slate or marble wainscot, or soapstone plastering for the walls around kitchen sink and laundry tubs to a height of four feet from floor, furnishing a complete non-absorbent wainscot impervious to moisture; or the bathroom wall entire may be tiled to a height of 5 feet from floor; or the sides and ends only of bathroom, on which plumbing is situated, may be tiled to a height of 4 to 5 feet, starting at door trim and ending at window trim. Or the entire bathroom may be plastered in a tinted soapstone non-absorbent plaster and polished plain or blocked off into tiling, in which case the carpenter will provide a neat rabbeted coping.

Drain Board for Kitchen Sink.

The carpenter will provide a drain board for kitchen sink of 1½-inch ash, supported on turned legs, resting on wheel castors; the top of drain board will be countersunk, dished and graded to drain and over-lap into kitchen sink. The top of drain board, should architect desire, may be constructed of soapstone, slate or dark Florentine marble, countersunk and dished, as above.

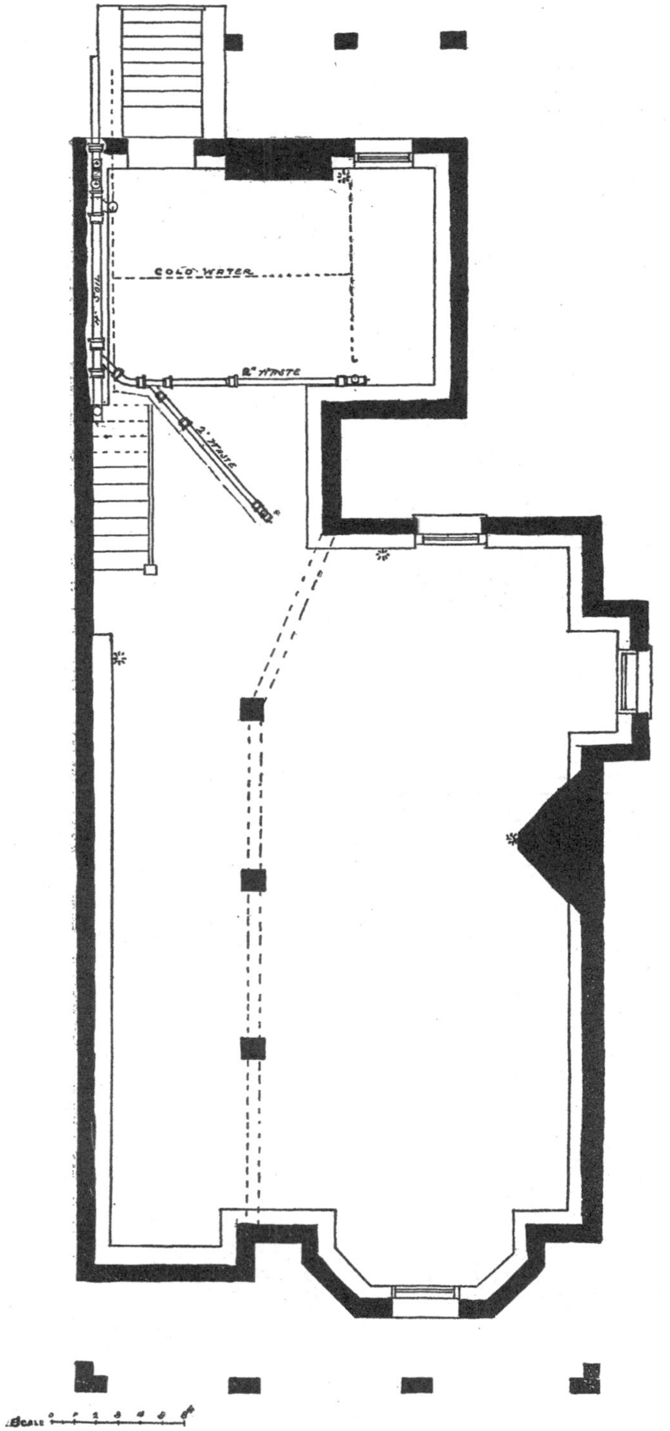

Plate I.

Suburban and Country Homes.

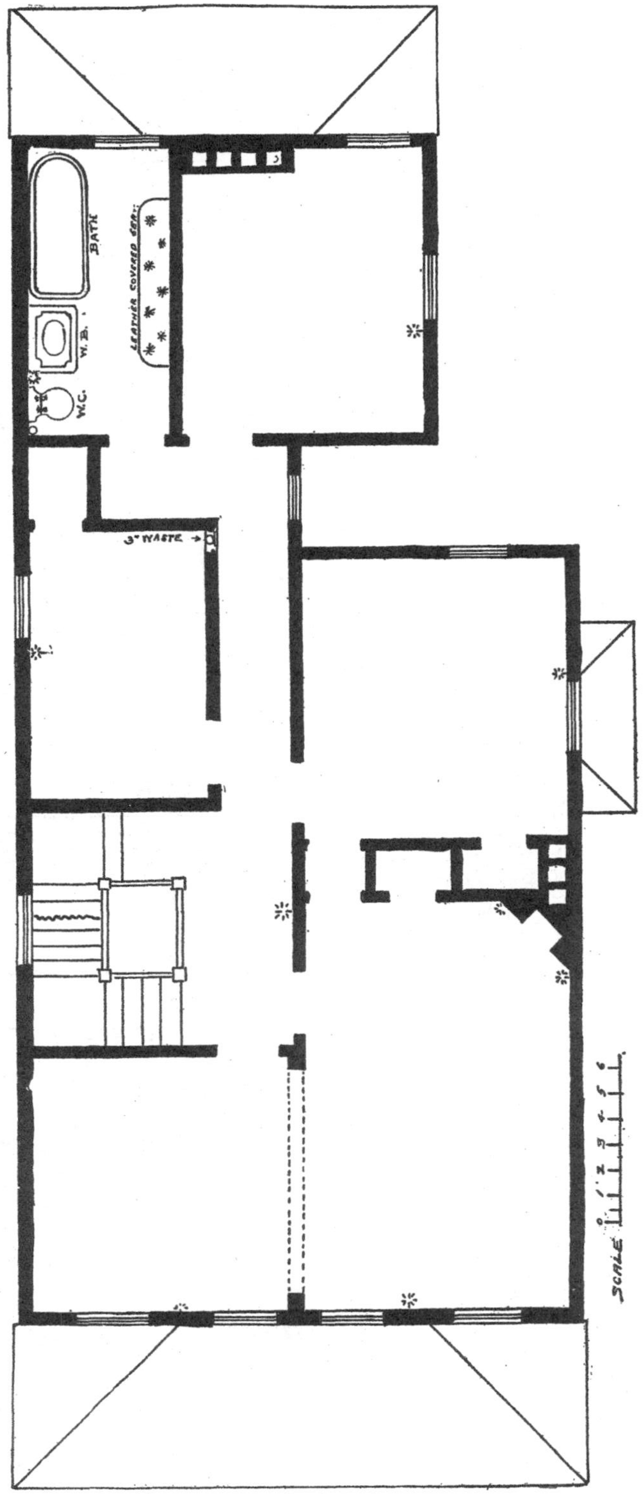

SECOND FLOOR.

FIRST FLOOR.

CELLAR.

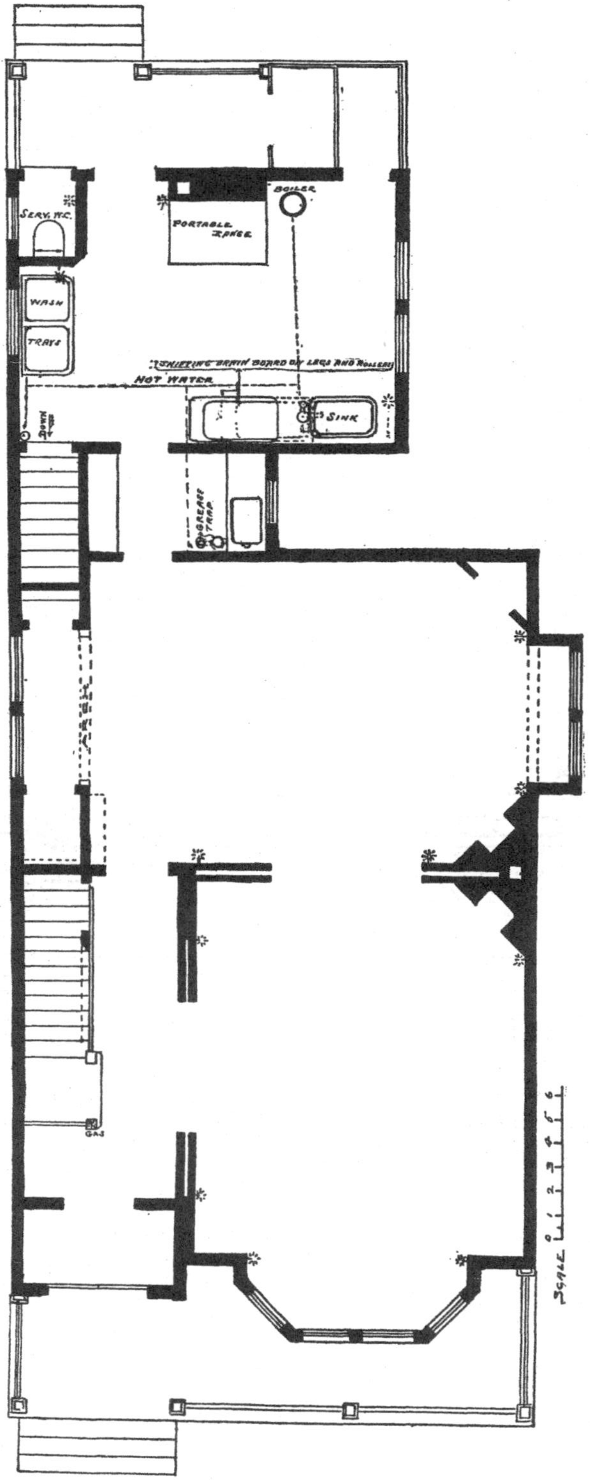

Plate II.

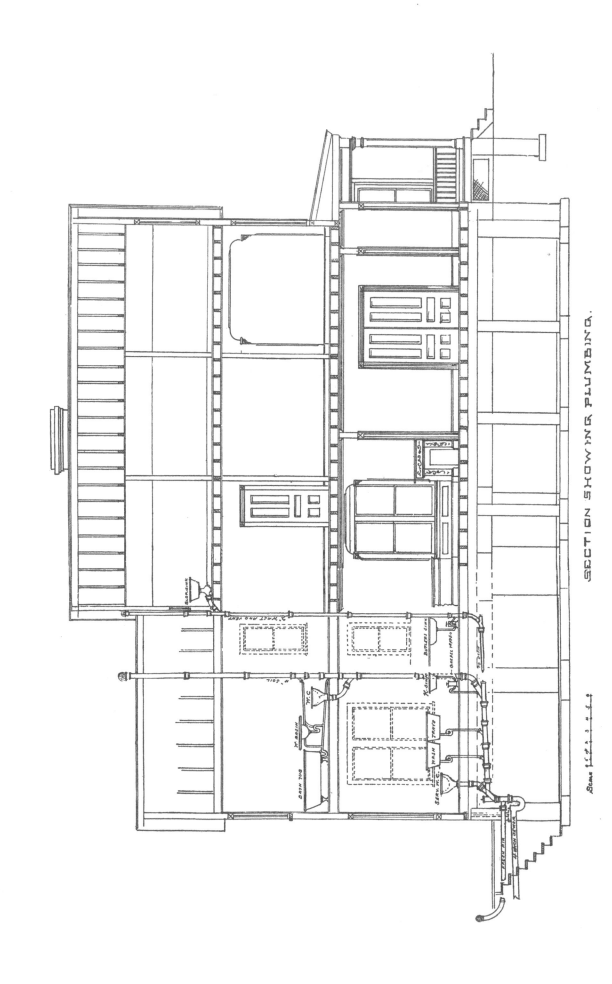

SECTION SHOWING PLUMBING.

PLATES III. AND IV.

THIS house is designed especially to meet the requirements of a small family desiring to enjoy the advantages of one of the many suburban towns surrounding our large cities, where narrow building lots are the rule, and is intended to give the greatest amount of actual comforts at least expense and to present a pleasing and attractive exterior, simple and chaste in character, such as the best taste indorses as befitting a family of small means.

The hall, by being roomy and comfortable, as well as unique in arrangement, is designed to make a cosy reception room for the casual caller, as well as a comfortable lounging place.

The plans, being simple and easily understood, need little or no explanation.

The exterior being covered entirely with shingles stained to give a gray roof and light brown walls, with trimmings painted in two shades of dark brown, would present a pleasing contrast. The interior finished in two shades of light tints could be made most homelike and tasteful.

An estimate of cost is appended that would vary slightly according to location and condition of local markets.

ESTIMATE OF COST.

Excavating and preliminary work	$ 40.00
Stone masonry	250.00
Brick masonry	100.00
Cement floor	50.00
Rough lumber, paper lining and shingles	450.00
Flooring lumber	80.00
Outside cornices, etc	20.00
Windows, doors and fittings	450.00
Other millwork	75.00
Stairways	100.00
Plumbing	200.00
Wiring for electric light and bells and fixtures	75.00
Mantels and fireplaces	75.00
Painting and glazing	225.00
Carpenter labor	300.00
Incidentals	100.00
Total	$2,590.00

Yarnall & Goforth
Architects
14 South Broad Street
Philadelphia, Pa.

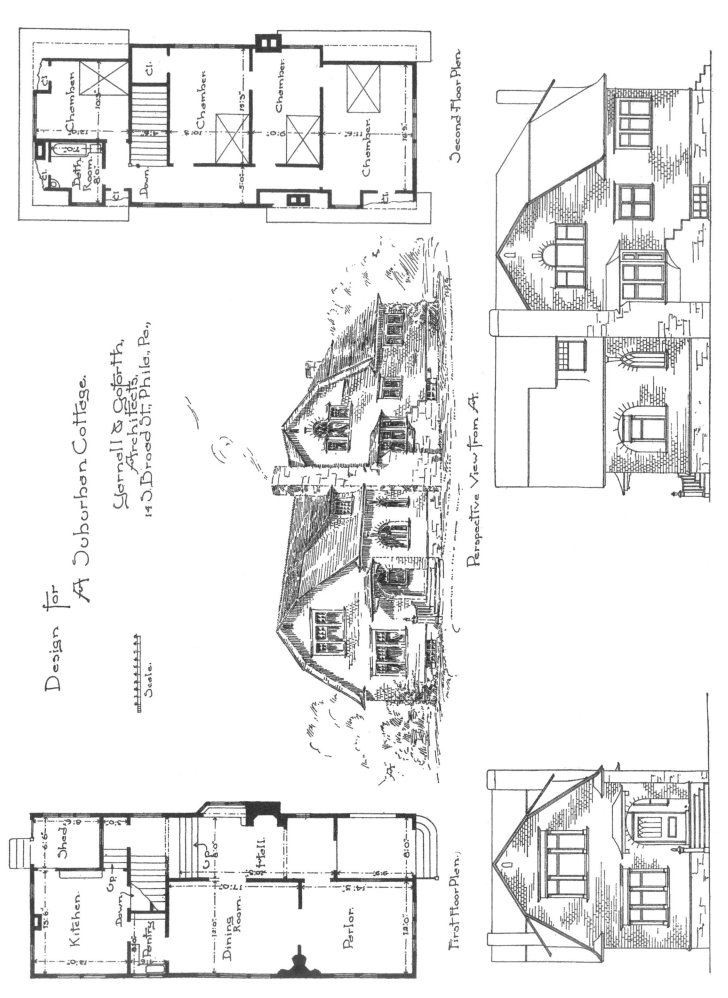

Suburban and Country Homes.

Plate III.

Design for A Suburban Cottage.

Yarnall & Goforth,
Architects,
14 S. Broad St., Phila., Pa.,

Scale.

Second Floor Plan.

Chamber

Ct.

Ct.

Bath. Room. 8'0"

Chamber

Chamber

Chamber

Chamber

Ct.

Perspective View from A.

Side Elevation.

First Floor Plan.

Kitchen.

Shed.

Pantry

Up.

Down.

Dining Room.

Hall.

Parlor.

Front Elevation.

Suburban and Country Homes.

Plate IV.

Design for

A Suburban Cottage.

Carnell & Scott,
Architects,
143 Broad St., Phila., Pa.

Scale

Side Elevation.

Rear Elevation.

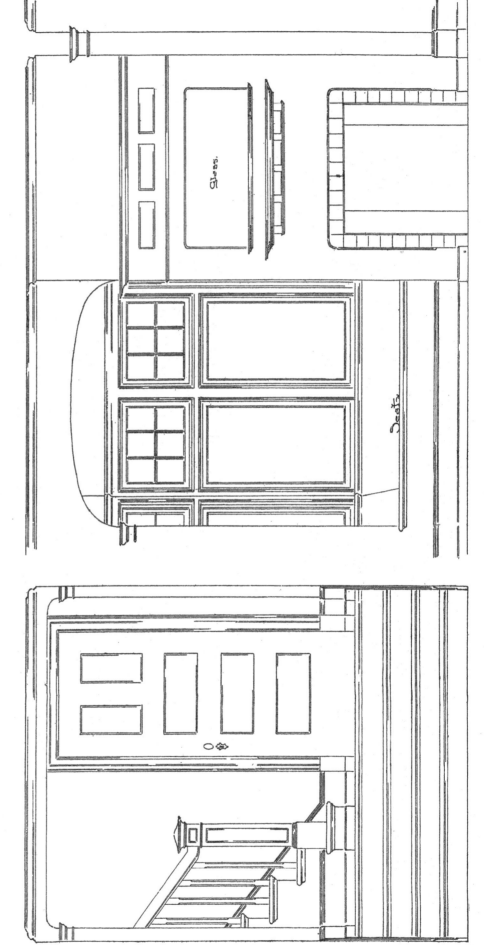

Glass.

Seat.

Detail of Bay and Fireplace.

Detail of Stairway.

PLATES V. AND VI.

THE perspective sketch, elevations and plans show an attractive design for a suburban home. The walls and roofs are shingled with white pine shingles. The stonework is carried up to sill height of bay, and shingled rail of porch is carried to ground, which give a more substantial effect than the ordinary lattice work.

The plans are very convenient and well arranged. There is a cemented cellar under the entire house, with walls of rock-faced stone. A good porch on front seven feet wide, and a kitchen porch on rear and outside blinds to windows.

There is an open fireplace in parlor, with tile facing and hearth and Colonial mantel with columns. Hard white plaster throughout building. Hard pine flooring on all floors. Whitewood trim, stained, in principal rooms. North Carolina pine trim, finished natural in all other rooms. Main staircase ash, and hall floored with ash for rugs. Front door ash glazed with beveled plate glass. Picture moulding in all rooms. Chair-rail in dining room and kitchen. Hall is lighted by art stained glass window. There are four bedrooms with good closets on second floor, and a convenient bathroom. A good staircase to attic, where there is one room finished, with space for two more. The butler's pantry is fitted up with counter, shelf and dresser, drawers, etc., complete. Bathroom is fitted with closet, bowl and bath. There is a sink in kitchen, and washtubs and servants' water closet in cellar. The cellar is reached by a stairway under the main flight and leading from the butler's pantry.

By placing the butler's pantry between the kitchen and dining room, and also between the hall and kitchen, the odor from cooking is prevented from reaching other parts of the house.

The height of ceilings are: Cellar, seven feet; first story, nine feet; second story, eight feet six inches; third story, seven feet six inches.

This house was recently built near Plainfield, N. J., with columns on porch in place of shingled arches, and pitched roof on bay instead of balustrade, otherwise as herein described, for $3,200 complete, including range, furnace and complete plumbing.

William A. Lambert
Architect
114 Nassau Street
New York.

Plate V.

Suburban and Country Homes.

WM. A. LAMBERT. ARCHITECT..
114 NASSAU ST. NEW YORK.

Plate VI.

Suburban and Country Homes.

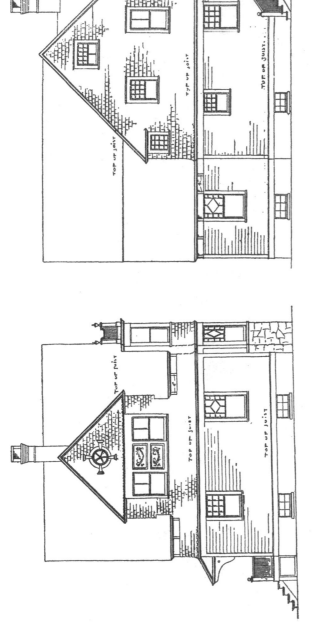

SIDE ELEVATION.

REAR ELEVATION.

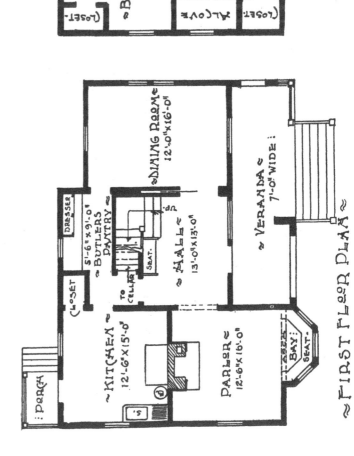

~ FIRST FLOOR PLAN ~

~ SECOND FLOOR PLAN ~

PLATES VII., VIII. AND IX.

A HOUSE of the following description has been built several times in various parts of the country, and varied in price from $4,400 to $5,100, according to location. These prices included heating, plumbing and mantels.

It must be understood that in general the cost given does not include papering, frescoing, gas or electric fixtures, lawn, gardening or fencing, which are matters usually left to the owner's taste as to style and expense, and not included in the contract for the erection of the building.

Hall and Staircase.
E.G.W.Dittrich-Architect
16 Broadway N.Y.

The design in this case contemplates the use of clapboards and shingles for the exterior covering, the whole standing upon a foundation of local stone. It will be noticed that the porches are carefully considered so as to insure a shady retreat from a torrid summer's day, at the same time not depriving the rooms of the necessary light. The rooms on the first floor are so arranged that they may readily be thrown together when desired. The large hall can be used for a sitting room. The arrangement of the staircase, enclosed in a bay with handsome leaded windows, seat and large open fireplace, with overhead beams, encased and fluted columns and composite capitals, is quite unique. The figures over the mantel are plaster and can be had in various designs, all ready to put up. The bricks in fireplace facing are intended for an old gold-colored brick and bluestone hearth. The wood is whitewood finished natural, and if the side walls and ceiling are tinted a light yellow with a simple stencil in a darker shade of the same color, the hall will be a very attractive feature of the house. The library is to be finished in natural whitewood, with fireplace facing of a dove-colored marble and dark blue tile hearth. The apple is used as a keynote for side walls and ceiling, starting with the apple red at the base board and shading it toward the ceiling into the apple green, with an apple green ceiling, walls and ceiling to have a simple design in olive green. The dining room is finished in whitewood stained a light color of

PLATES VII., VIII. AND IX.—*Continued.*

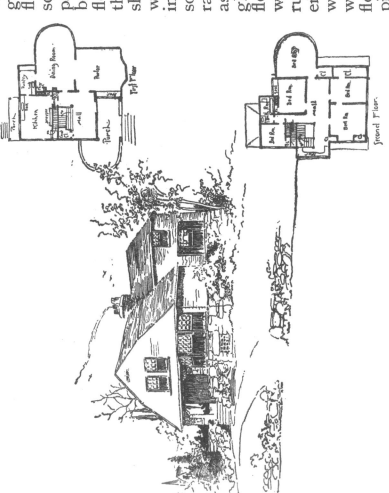

walnut, with side walls painted in glazed colors. Taking the golden rod flower as a keynote for the color scheme, stenciled with a flat color of pale yellow, the glazed color should be graded from the dark yellow in the flower to the palest color, starting from the top of the paneled wainscot and shading into the centre of ceiling, the wood cornice in angle of ceiling breaking the color so as not to become tiresome. The china closets are so arranged that the lower part can be used as a sideboard, with beveled plate glass doors above for the china. The flooring on first floor to be yellow pine, waxed and covered with old Turkish rugs. The parlor is painted in cream enamel and the side walls are papered with a paper that resembles a fine woven material covered with a small flower, the ceiling to be tinted a pale pink, stenciled. The kitchen is arranged to have all modern improvements. The woodwork is finished with spar varnish. This does not mar or spot if water gets on it, or if scratched lightly it does not show. A back stairway reaches the second floor from the kitchen. A large pantry separates the kitchen from the dining room, with cases, shelving and sink. A storeroom provided with shelving gives ample room for laying in supplies. A coat closet is also provided and answers as a passageway. The cellar is divided up into furnace room, coal and wood bins, vegetable cellar and laundry, with stationary washtubs and servants' water closet. The second floor shows four good bedrooms; the third or attic floor contains two large bedrooms, with closets and a good trunk room. All the plumbing work is open.

E. G. W. Dietrich
Architect
18 Broadway
New York

Plate VII.

Suburban and Country Homes.

Sketch for House at
Ashville, N. C.
E. G. W. Dietrich, Architect
13 Broadway, New York, N. Y.

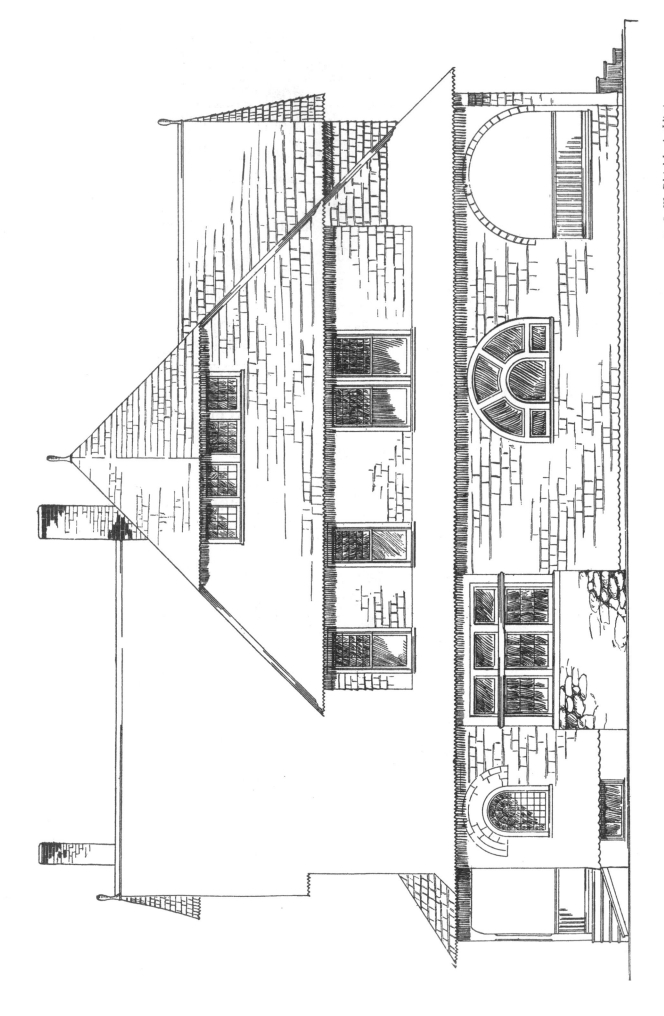

Plate VIII.

Suburban and Country Homes.

Side Elevation.

E. G. W. Dietrich, Architect
18 Broadway, New York

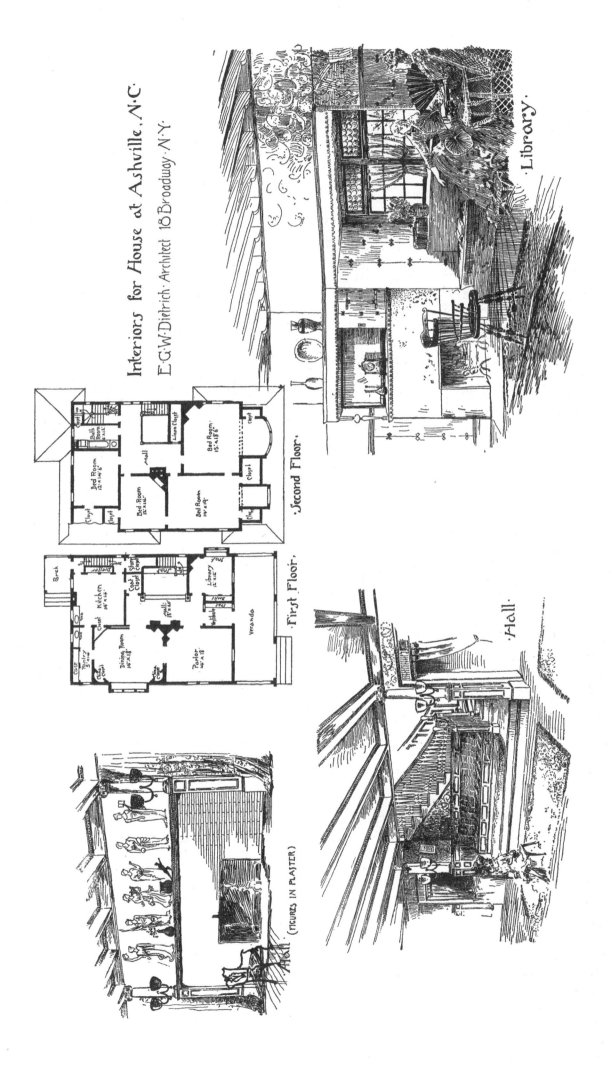

Plate IX.

Suburban and Country Homes.

Interiors for House at Ashville. N.C.

E.G.W. Dietrich. Architect 18 Broadway. N.Y.

First Floor.

Second Floor.

Library.

Hall.

(FIGURES IN PLASTER)

PLATE X.

THE perspective view of this house will be found in the Frontispiece. Plate X. shows the elevations, plans and a section of stairs in hall. It is a frame house, with exterior walls and roof shingled with cedar "clears" stained with gray shingle stain and trimmings painted warm white.

The cellar wall is built of local stone, laid in cement mortar, smoothly plastered on outside to resist action of frost, the house being designed for the climate of northern New England.

The cellar floor is cemented. The laundry is finished under kitchen. The kitchen and pantries are finished in whitewood, filled and coated with waterproof varnish. Bathroom finished in the same' manner, but all other rooms finished in painted pine.

The dining room has paneled wainscot five feet high; ceiling paneled on plaster, with moulded wooden ribs. One room is finished in attic; remainder of space left with a good single floor.

Kitchen, back entry, pantries and bathroom have painted walls, but all other rooms on first and second floors have walls papered and ceilings tinted to correspond. Birch floors for hall, dining room, kitchen, back entries, pantries and bathrooms. All else of good dry spruce for carpet.

The exterior stonework shown is laid in rough rubble with mortar joints kept back from face; stone laid with natural face exposed.

The fireplaces are of good face-bricks in red mortar with "Murdock" throats and unglazed tile hearths. The house is heated by hot air.

This house was built in Maine substantially as shown (though under somewhat exceptional circumstances) for a little more than $4,ooo. It should be easily built for $5,ooo if carried out in the manner indicated above.

John Calvin Stevens
Architect
Oxford Building
Portland, Me.

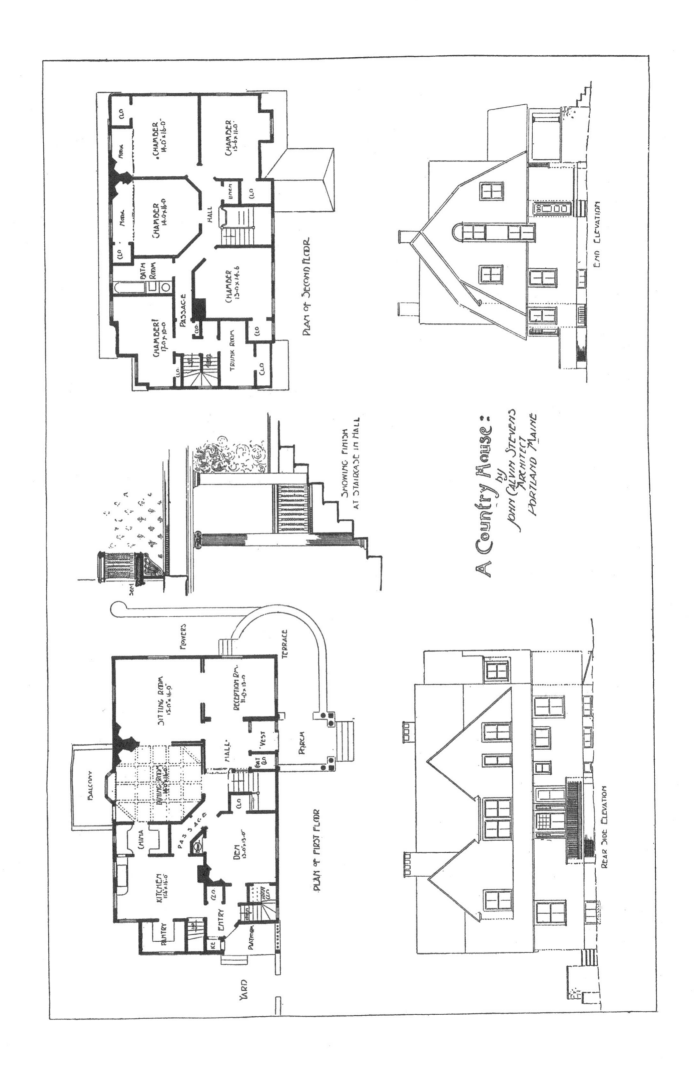

Suburban and Country Homes.

Plate X.

PLATE XI.

THIS cosy little house is designed to meet the requirements of a small family. The first floor contains a living room, bedroom and kitchen, with a large pantry between kitchen and living room, a porch in front and a small porch in rear. The second floor has three bedrooms. The exterior is covered with shingles stained a silver gray, with trimmings painted white, the whole presenting a very artistic effect. The interior is finished in natural whitewood throughout. All rooms connect with the hall. Cellar under entire house. Cost, $1,500 complete.

Manly N. Cutter
Architect
203 Broadway
New York

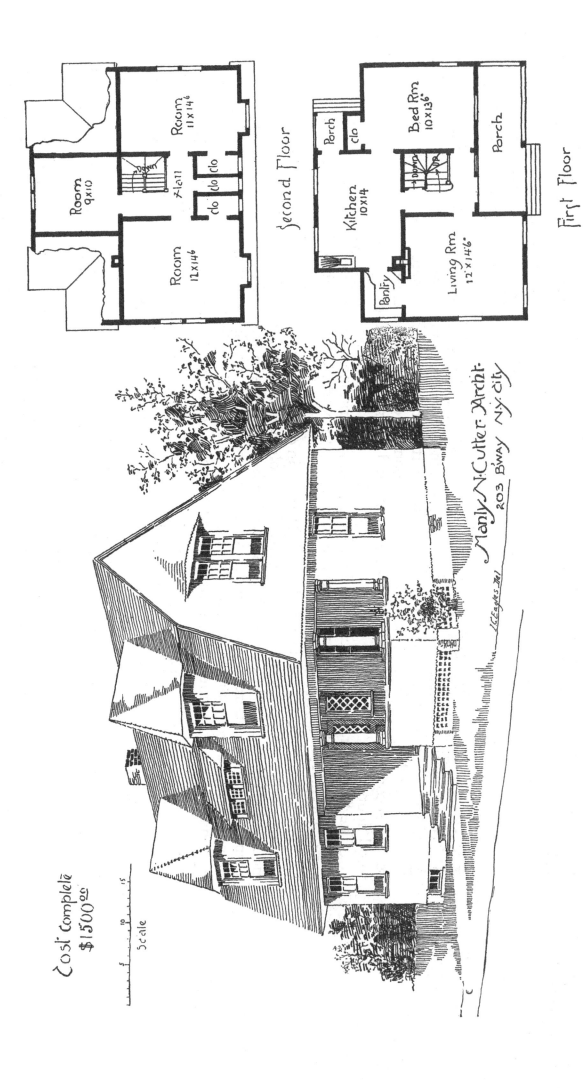

Plate XI.

Suburban and Country Homes.

Room 9x10

Room 11x14⁶

Hall

clo clo

clo clo

Down

Room 12x14⁶

Second Floor

Porch

clo

Bed Rm 10x13⁶

Kitchen 10x14

Pantry

Living Rm 12'x14⁶"

Porch

First Floor

Manly N. Cutter Archt. 203 B'way N.Y. City

J.C.Edgers Del.

Cost complete $1500⁰⁰

Scale

PLATE XII.

IN this design the aim has been to get as many large rooms as possible conveniently accessible. A hall, drawing room or parlor, dining room, kitchen, butler's pantry and closets constitute the first floor, while there are four large bedrooms, a good-sized bathroom and numerous closets on the second floor. The halls, drawing room and dining room have hard-wood floors.

The first floor, except kitchen and butler's pantry, is trimmed with white-wood, stained. All the other rooms are trimmed with North Carolina pine, finished natural.

The hall is about 14x19 feet and has a fireplace in one end. The chimney is built of pressed brick, exposed to view the whole height of ceiling. The moulded shelf rests on brick corbels. A paneled beam crosses in front of the chimney, from the staircase to the partition, resting on carved brackets at the ends, making a very pretty feature of this end of the hall. There is a stationary seat at the side of the stairs. The drawing and dining rooms open into the hall by sliding doors.

The ceilings of the first and second floors are nine feet six inches and eight feet six inches high respectively.

The walls of the halls, drawing and dining rooms are sand finished and tinted. Other walls are white hard finish. The plumbing fixtures are of the best. The laundry is in the cellar and has stationary tubs. The house is heated with a hot air furnace. The entire exterior is covered with shingles, stained.

Estimated cost, $5,000; but does not include heating, mantels and leaded glass.

Theodore Hopping
Architect
28 South Willow Street
Montclair, N.J.

Plate XII.

Suburban and Country Homes.

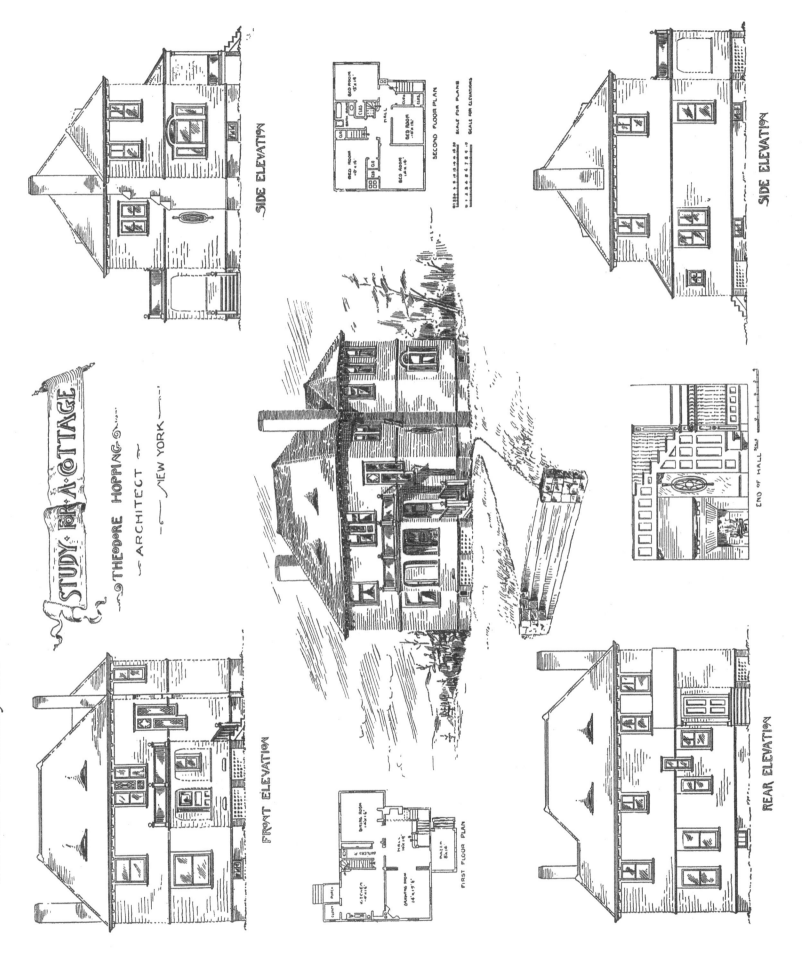

SIDE ELEVATION

SECOND FLOOR PLAN

SCALE FOR PLANS

SCALE FOR ELEVATIONS

SIDE ELEVATION

STUDY · FOR · A · COTTAGE

THEODORE HOPPING

ARCHITECT

NEW YORK

END OF HALL

FRONT ELEVATION

FIRST FLOOR PLAN

REAR ELEVATION

PLATES XIII. AND XIV.

THIS house is exceedingly well planned in first and second stories as to convenience, size and number of rooms.

The laundry is in the cellar under the kitchen, and in the attic are two servants' rooms. The staircase is so arranged that back stairs are considered unnecessary and are omitted in the cost.

The exterior walls of the house are covered with clapboards, mitred at corners on second story, and the roof with pine shingles on strips.

All detail, both interior and exterior, is of a simple Colonial character, as shown. The staircase is of white pine, with cherry rail; the floors are double, the upper ones being of North Carolina pine; fireplaces are finished with brick facings, and all mantels, china closet, etc., are of white pine or whitewood.

The plastering generally has a sand finish, and all woodwork, both interior and exterior, has three coats of paint, or its equivalent in wood filler, stain and oil or varnish.

This house, simply, neatly and completely finished, is estimated to cost $5,000.

E. L. Messenger
Architect
New York
and
29 Prospect Place
Brooklyn, N. Y.

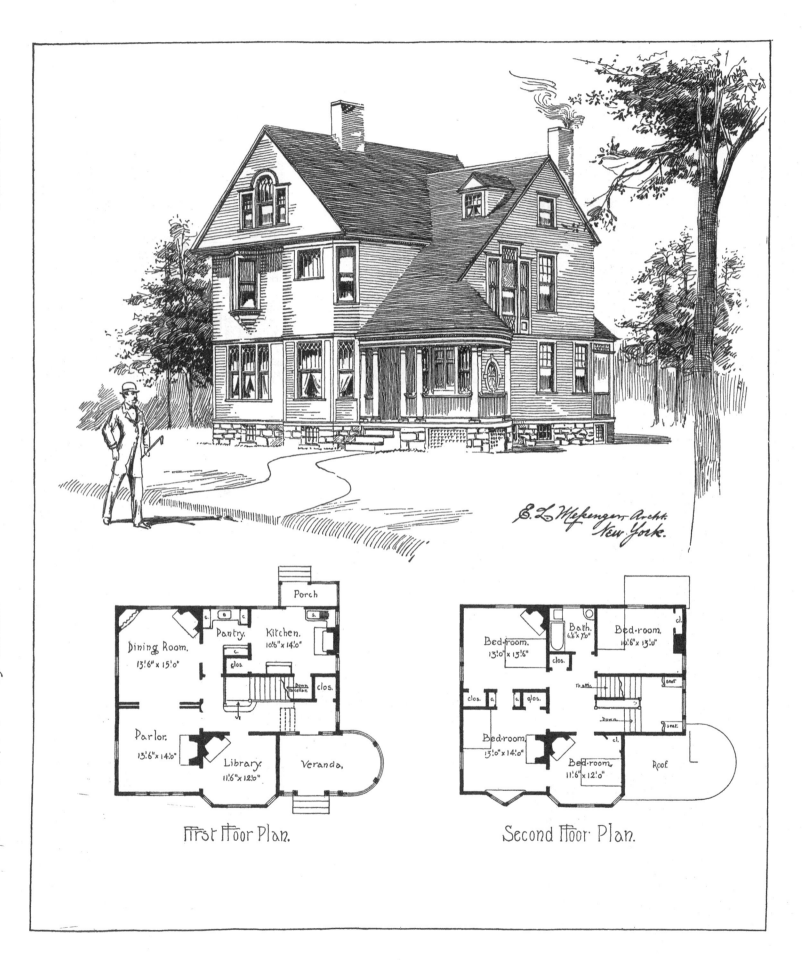

Plate XIII.

E. L. Wesenger, Archt.
New York.

First Floor Plan.

Second Floor Plan.

Dining Room.
13'6" x 15'0"

Pantry.

Kitchen.
10'6" x 14'0"

clos.

clos.

Down to cellar.

Parlor.
13'6" x 14'0"

Library.
11'6" x 12'0"

Veranda.

Porch.

Bath.
6'6" x 7'6"

Bed-room.
13'0" x 13'6"

Bed-room.
10'6" x 13'0"

clos.

To attic.

clos.

clos.

seat.

Down.

seat.

Bed-room.
13'0" x 14'0"

Bed-room.
11'6" x 12'0"

Roof.

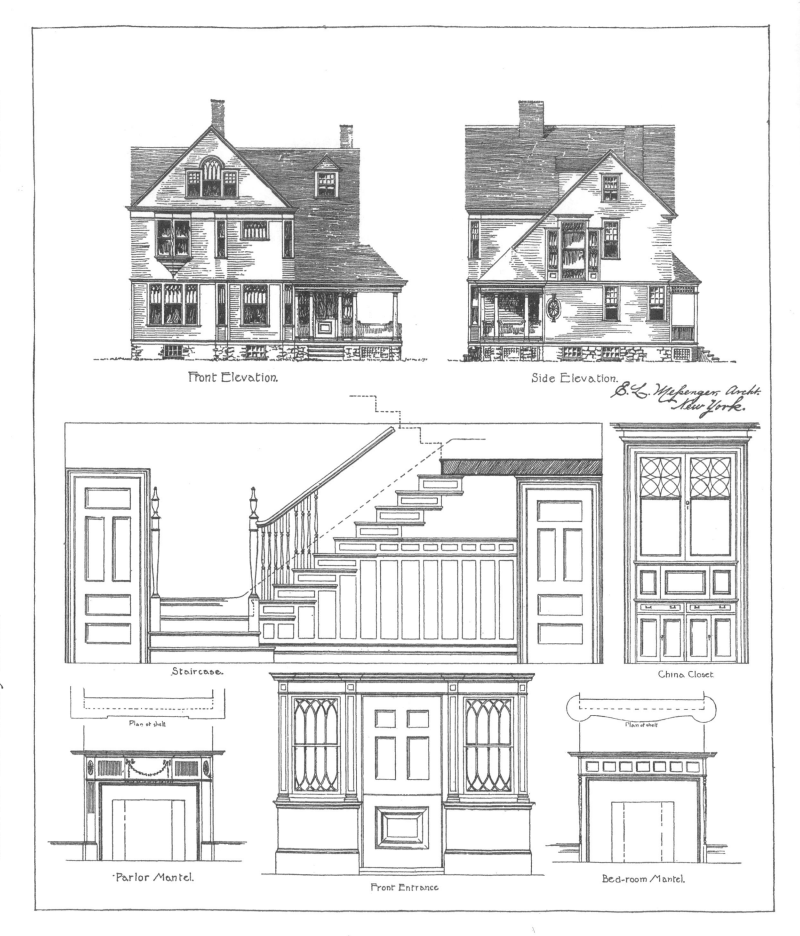

Plate XIV.

Suburban and Country Homes.

Front Elevation.

Side Elevation.

B. L. Messenger, Archt.
New York.

Staircase.

China Closet.

Plan of shelf

Parlor Mantel.

Front Entrance

Plan of shelf

Bed-room Mantel.

PLATE XV.

THIS design is planned to contain a music room or parlor, dining room and kitchen on first floor, with large verandas in front and rear. The second floor has three bedrooms and bathroom; one of the bedrooms has an alcove. The interior finish is of North Carolina pine and whitewood, stained to suit. All rooms plastered. The exterior is covered with cedar shingles stained in one tint, graded from roof down. The plumbing is simple and of best quality. Cellar under whole house. Estimated cost, $4,500.

George Martin Huss
Architect
1285 Broadway
New York

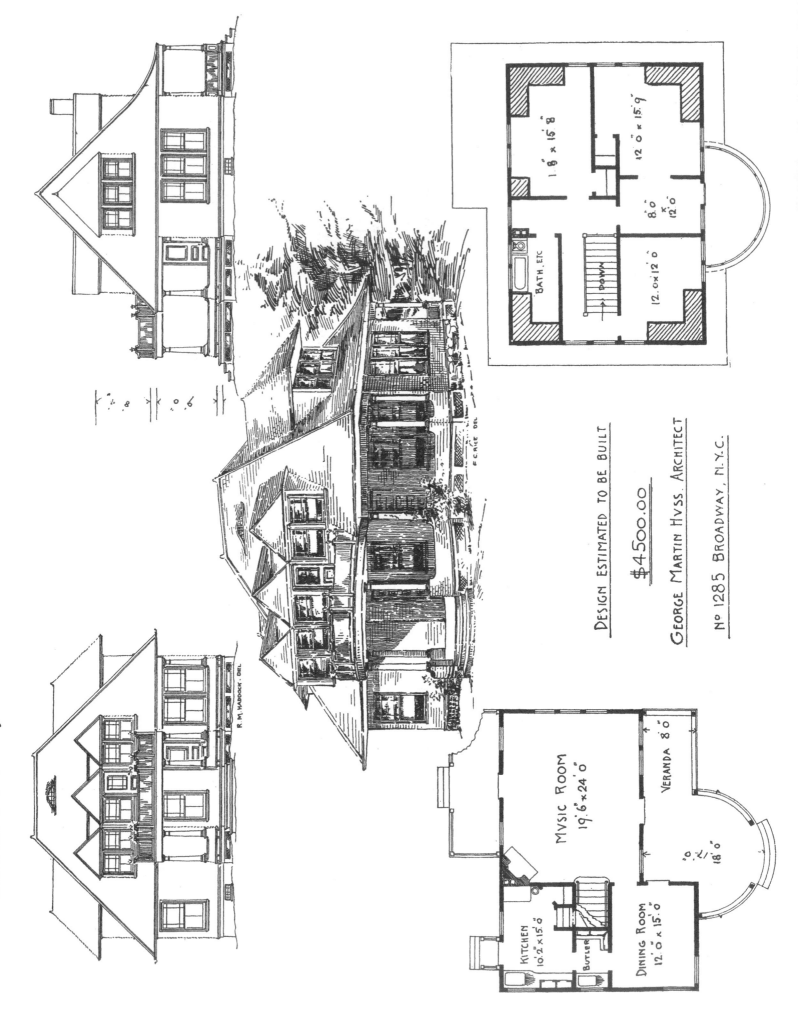

Plate XV.

Suburban and Country Homes.

R. M. HADDOCK · DEL.

F. CASE DEL.

DESIGN ESTIMATED TO BE BUILT

$4500.00

GEORGE MARTIN HVSS ARCHITECT

Nᵒ 1285 BROADWAY, N.Y.C.

BATH, ETC

12 0 × 12 0

1 8 × 15 8

8 0
12 0

12 0 × 15 9

MVSIC ROOM
19 6 × 24 0

VERANDA 8 0

18 0

KITCHEN
10 2 × 15 0

BUTLER

DINING ROOM
12 0 × 15 0

PLATES XVI. AND XVII.

ENTRANCE DOOR.
HOUSE AT FOREST MILL, N. J.
CHARLES P. BALDWIN, ARCHITECT

HIS house was erected at Forest Hill, N. J., and contains on the first floor a parlor, library, reception hall, dining room and kitchen; also a covered porch in front. The second floor has four large bedrooms and a bathroom, together with ample closet room. The exterior is covered with white pine sawed shingles of different widths, stained a light old gold, with courses of saw-toothed work. The roof is also shingled and stained a dark moss green. All casings, doors, cornices, sash, etc., of exterior are painted a cream white.

The interior trimmings are of selected whitewood, natural finish. Cellar under whole house. All rooms have plastered walls, with ceilings tinted in water colors, except in kitchen and bathroom, which are hard oil finished. Each room is finished in three colors and no two alike, parlor in cream, dining room in chocolate, sage green and cream, hall in sage green, copper, red and cream, and library in salmon pinks.

ESTIMATE OF COST.—Carpenter work, $2,440; mason work, $830; plumbing and heating, $470; painting, $300. Total, $4,040.

Charles P. Baldwin
Architect
Prudential Building
Newark, N. J.

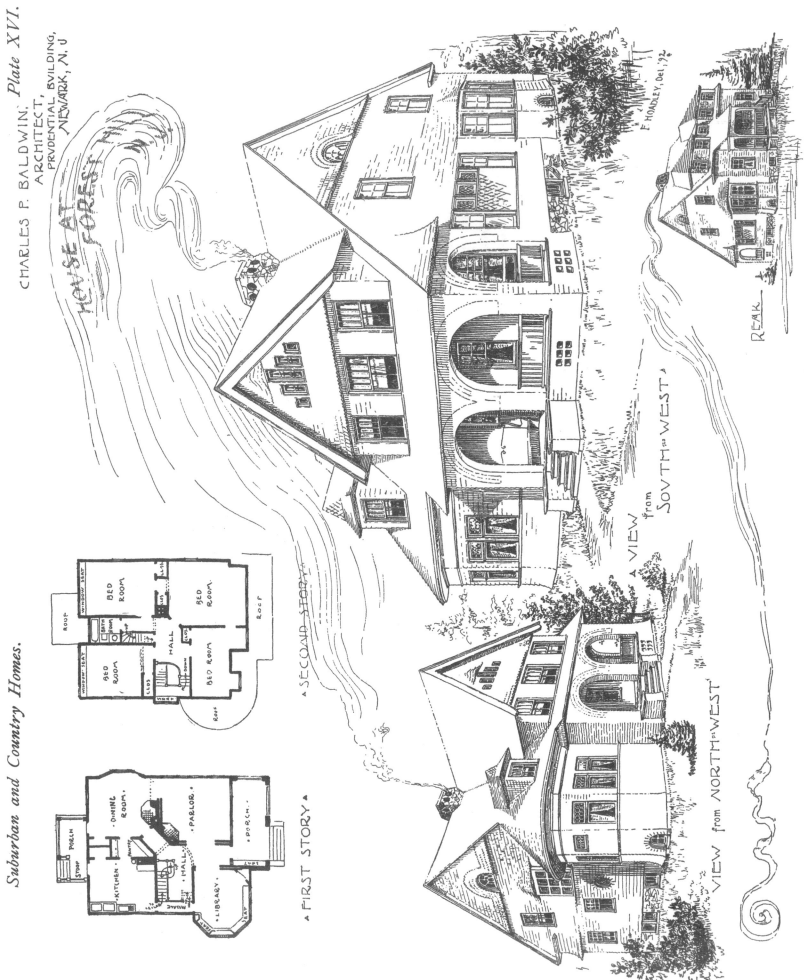

Suburban and Country Homes.

CHARLES P. BALDWIN, Architect.
PRVDENTIAL BVILDING,
NEWARK, N. J.

Plate XVI.

HOUSE AT FOREST

F. HOADLEY, Oct, '92

A VIEW from SOUTH-WEST.

VIEW from NORTH-WEST.

REAR.

FIRST STORY

SECOND STORY

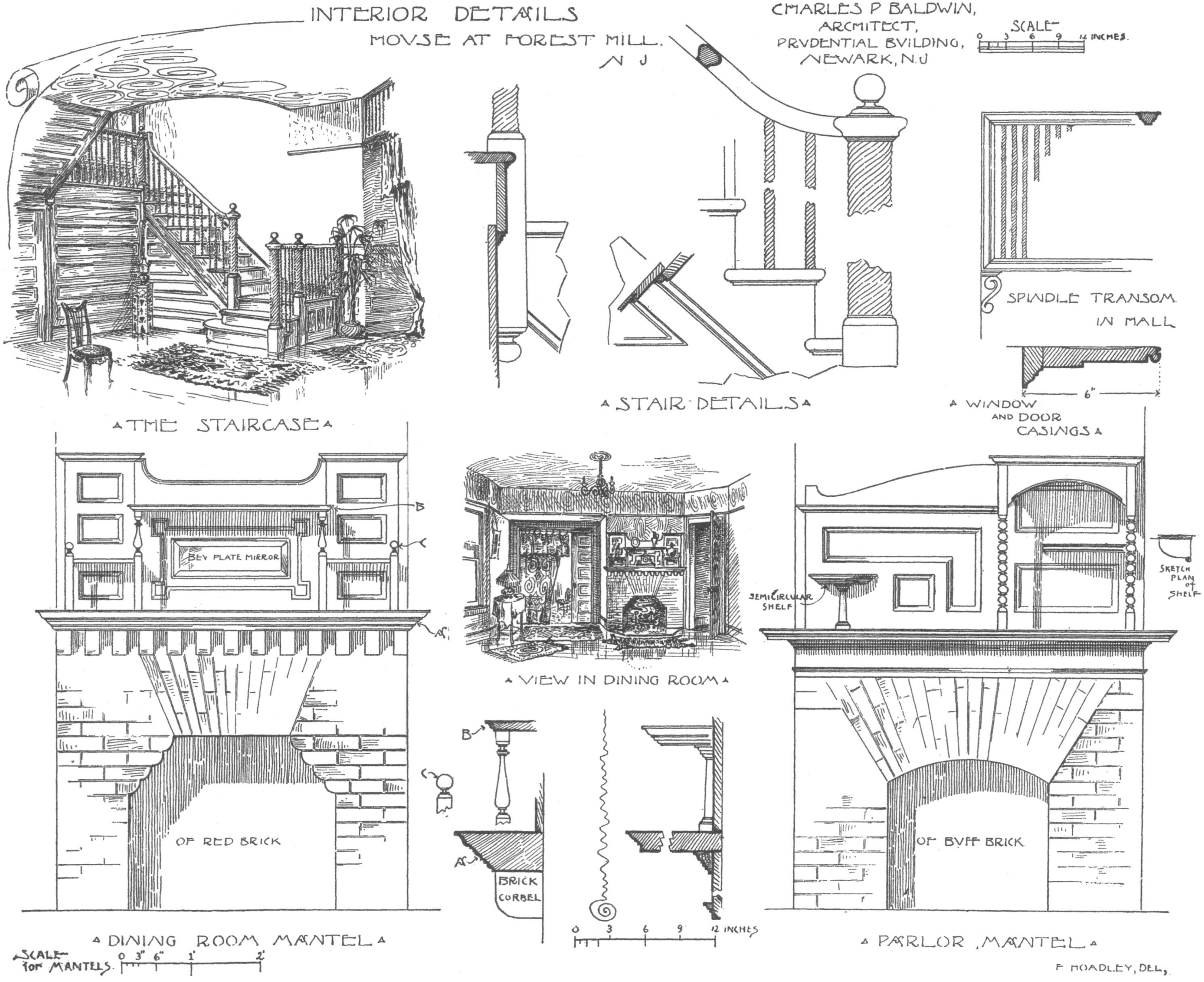

Suburban and Country Homes.

Plate XVII.

INTERIOR DETAILS

HOVSE AT FOREST MILL.
N J

CHARLES P BALDWIN,
ARCHITECT,
PRVDENTIAL BVILDING,
NEWARK, N.J

SCALE
0 3 6 9 12 INCHES.

▲ SPINDLE TRANSOM
IN HALL

6"

▲ WINDOW
AND DOOR
CASINGS ▲

SKETCH
PLAN
OF
SHELF

▲ STAIR DETAILS ▲

SEMICIRCULAR
SHELF

OF BVFF BRICK

▲ PARLOR MANTEL ▲

F. ROADLEY, DEL,

▲ VIEW IN DINING ROOM ▲

0 3 6 9 12 INCHES

B

BRICK
CORBEL

A

▲ THE STAIRCASE ▲

B

BEV PLATE MIRROR

OF RED BRICK

▲ DINING ROOM MANTEL ▲

SCALE
fOR MANTELS 0 3' 6" 1' 2'

PLATE XVIII.

A HOUSE suitable for a suburban town, where narrow building lots are the rule, is here presented. The house has a frontage of twenty-one feet and is arranged to contain on the first floor a hall, parlor, dining room and kitchen, with butler's pantry, also a piazza across the front. The second floor has three bedrooms, with ample closets and bathroom. The front bedroom has a large circular bay and an alcove for the bed. The first story is built of brick laid in red mortar, and the second story and attic of open timber work and cement. The cellar is under entire house, and contains the laundry and furnace. The hall is finished in oak, with spindle arch to parlor; parlor in cherry, dining room in antique oak and kitchen in Georgia pine.

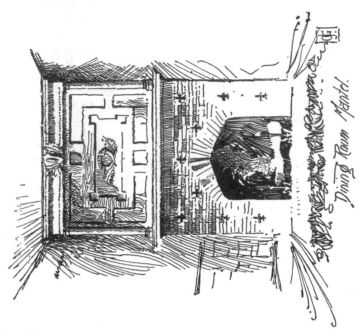

Dining Room Mantel.

The Entrance.

Otto J. Gette
Architect
378 Sackett Street
Brooklyn, N. Y.

Plate XVIII.

Design for a Suburban House
on a 25 ft Lot

Otto J Gette
Architect del

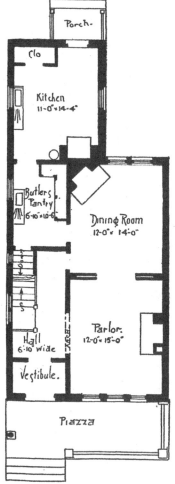

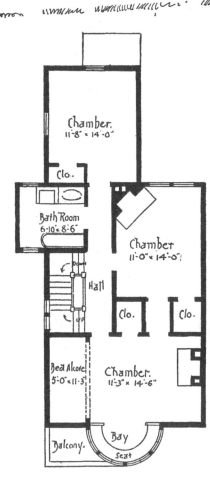

FIRST STORY.

Porch.

Clo

Kitchen
11'-0" × 14'-4"

Butlers
Pantry
6'-10" × 10'-0"

Dining Room
12'-0" × 14'-0"

Hall
6'-10" wide

Parlor
12'-0" × 15'-0"

Vestibule.

Piazza

SECOND STORY.

Chamber.
11'-8" × 14'-0"

Clo.

Bath Room
6'-10" × 8'-6"

Chamber
11'-0" × 14'-0"

Hall

Clo.

Clo.

Bed Alcove
5'-0" × 11'-3"

Chamber.
11'-3" × 14'-6"

Balcony.

Bay
Seat

REAR ELEVATION.

PLATES XIX. AND XX.

I T was the aim in designing this cottage to make a convenient, economical and artistic house suitable for a suburban home of a family of moderate means. The design embodies a picturesque exterior and a convenient interior. There is a good cellar under entire building, seven feet deep, with walls built of rock-faced quarry stone, containing laundry and servants' water closet. The porch on front is of good size, the circular part being very effective. The hall will be floored with ash, and platform staircase of ash with turned and fluted newels, spindle balusters and cosy seat. The hall is lighted by art stained glass windows. The parlor has a large corner bay and sliding doors connecting with dining room. It is finished in white and gold with pretty Colonial mantel finished in same way.

Dining room has an open fireplace, with tile hearth and facings, attractive cabinet mantel and large bay window. The butler's pantry is placed between the dining room and kitchen, and has double swinging doors. It is fitted up with dresser, drawers and small closet. The kitchen is provided with range, sink and all the usual fixtures.

It has a back staircase and stairs to cellar and fair-sized porch. There are four bedrooms on second floor, each provided with ample closets. The bathroom is wainscoted and fitted up with embossed closet, oval decorated wash bowl and bath.

There is a good staircase to attic, where there is space to finish two rooms. The trim of dining room and halls is whitewood. Hard pine, finished natural, in all other rooms.

Front door is glazed with art stained glass. Picture moulding in all rooms. Hard pine flooring on all floors except hall. The entire building is sheathed with hemlock boards and built in a thorough manner. It is heated by a hot air furnace. This house was recently built as above described.

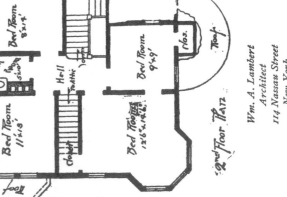

Wm. A. Lambert
Architect
114 Nassau Street
New York

Suburban and Country Homes.

Plate XIX.

WM. A. LAMBERT
ARCHITECT
114 NASSAU ST N.Y.

Plate XX.

Suburban and Country Homes.

PLATE XXI.

THIS entire house is to be shingled with cedar shingles; those on the side walls to be stained with creosote stain, either gray or buff, and all trim to be painted white. The roof to be untreated and to take the natural weather stain. The interior to be trimmed in soft wood, either whitewood or pine, and stained, finished natural color or painted, according to the taste of the owner. The staircase to be hardwood, as also the mantels. One room finished in the attic. The house can be built in good substantial manner, complete, for $5,000.

Stanley S. Covert
Architect
19 Park Place
New York

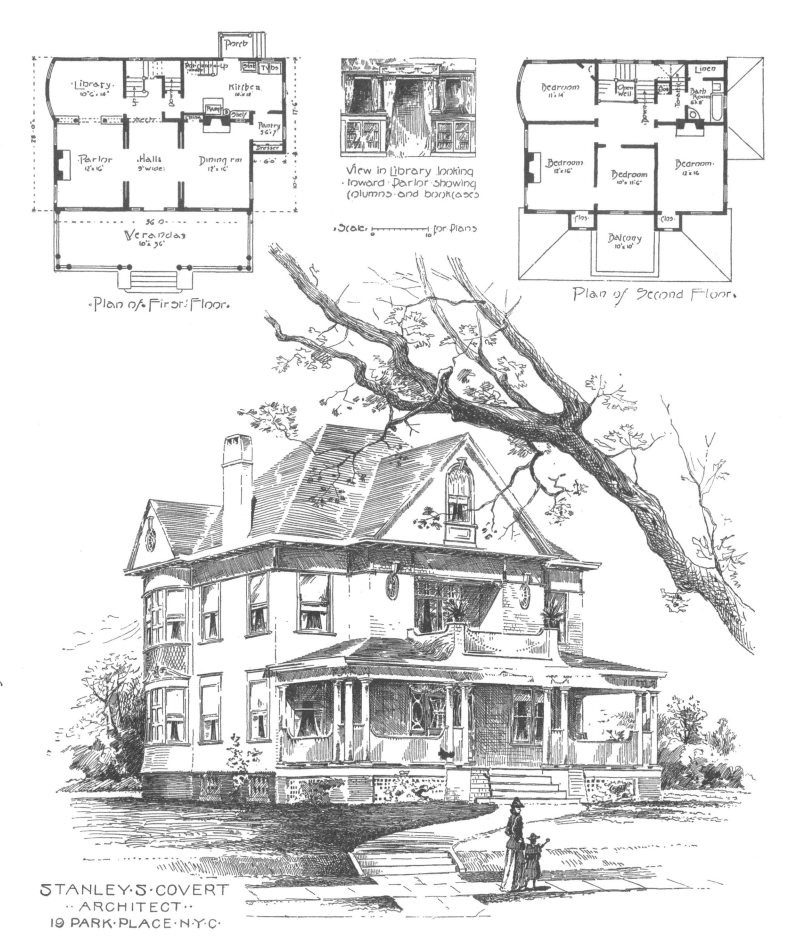

Plate XXI.

Library
10'6" x 14'

Kitchen
10 x 18

Porch

Sink Tubs

up

Parlor
12' x 16'

Halls
9' wide

Dining rm
12' x 16'

Pantry
5'6" x 7'

Shelf

Dresser

6'-0"

56'-0"

28'-0"

17'-6"

10'-6"

Verandas
10' x 36'

Plan of First Floor.

View in Library looking
toward Parlor showing
columns and bookcases

Scale ——————— for Plans
0   10

Bedroom
11 x 14

Open
Well

Linen

Bath
Room
6'x8'

Toilet

Down

Bedroom
12' x 16'

Bedroom
10'x 11'6"

Bedroom
12' x 16'

Clos.

Clos.

Balcony
10' x 10'

Plan of Second Floor.

Suburban and Country Homes.

STANLEY·S·COVERT
··ARCHITECT··
19 PARK·PLACE·N·Y·C·

PLATES XXII. AND XXIII.

A SOMEWHAT novel idea is here presented of a house designed for a corner lot having a frontage of twenty feet, with stable, barn and residence under one roof. The first floor has a large veranda in front, a reception room, dining room and kitchen. In the rear is situated the stable, with carriage house, two stalls, harness room and a large stable-yard. The second floor contains three chambers, servants' room and store-room. The exterior is covered with shingles, stained. The cellar walls are of rubble stone and the chimneys of stone and brick. The interior is finished in hardwood, with floors of Southern pine. Cellar and stable-yard are concreted. Estimated cost, including plumbing and electric bells, $4,600.

L. S. Buffington
Architect
Minneapolis, Minn.

Suburban and Country Homes.

Plate XXII.

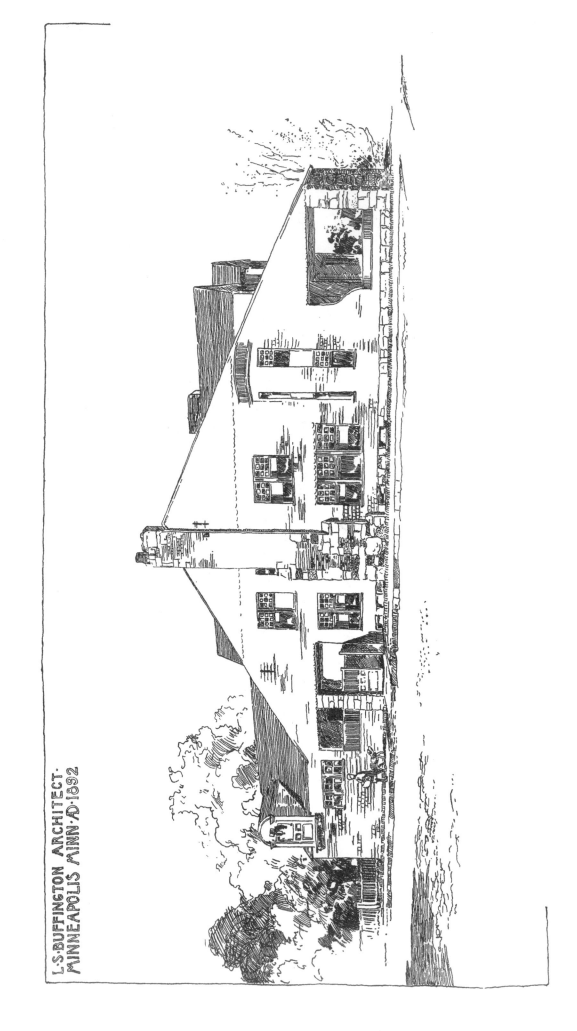

L.S.BUFFINGTON ARCHITECT.
MINNEAPOLIS MINN. A·D·1892

Plate XXIII.

Suburban and Country Homes.

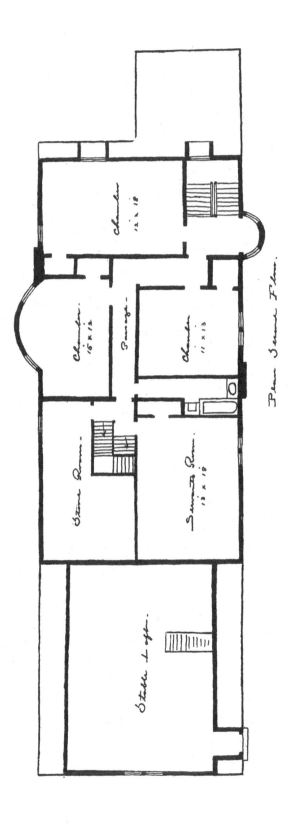

Plan Second Floor.

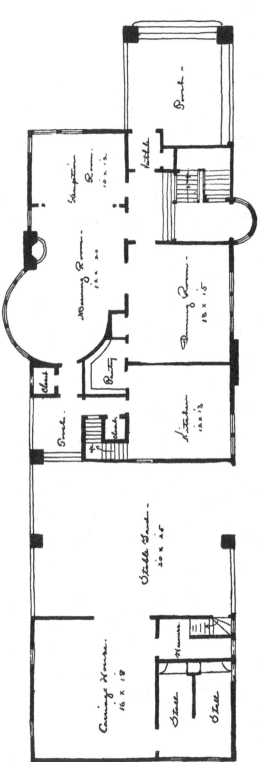

Plan of First Floor.

PLATE XXIV.

THIS house is to be built of white Roman tile, with stone trimmings. Dimensions in clear are 44x28 feet; heights of stories are: first floor, nine feet six inches, and of second floor eight feet six inches.

The roof is covered with red cedar shingles, stained brown. The trim throughout the interior is of whitewood and oak; all trim in hall and dining room is of oak, finished in antique.

The hall contains an ornamental staircase, with turned and carved newel and balusters; also a large open fireplace, built of English tiles. Dining room and library have similar fireplaces, also built of tiles.

Butler's pantry contains dressers, closets, sink, etc. Kitchen and kitchen pantry are wainscoted in Georgia pine and fitted up complete.

There are four large bedrooms, one dressing room and a good-sized bathroom, with closets for each room on second floor. Large billiard room in attic, and basement has cemented floor, furnace, laundry and servants' bathroom.

Bills of material: Common brick, 68,000; Roman tile, 10,000. Stone, 124 feet 8x5-inch sills; 14 feet of 24x8-inch cap; 20 feet of 8x5-inch transom; three chimney caps; 40 feet coping, 14x5 inches; 148 feet footing, 17x8 inches. Lumber, first story, 20 pieces 2x12 inches by 24 feet long; 22 pieces 2x12 inches by 14 feet long. Second story, 20 pieces 2x10 inches by 24 feet long; 22 pieces 2x10 inches by 14 feet long. Ceiling joists, 20 pieces 2x8 inches by 24 feet long; 22 pieces 2x8 inches by 14 feet long. Roof, 84 pieces 2x6 inches by 18 feet long. First story studs, 103 pieces 2x4 inches by 9 feet 6 inches long. Second story studs, 120 pieces 2x4 inches by 8 feet 6 inches long. Plaster, 800 yards; flooring, 3,500 feet; sheathing, 1,500 feet; shingles, 18 squares; 25 doors; 23 windows; oak staircase, 3 pine staircases; plumbing, $350; 3 dormer windows. Hardware, solid bronze, $150; gutters, flashings, etc., $25.

Brackets and porch posts of whitewood. Cornices open showing "jack" rafters. Estimated cost, $5,000.

McCurdy & Pulis
Architects
Denver, Col.

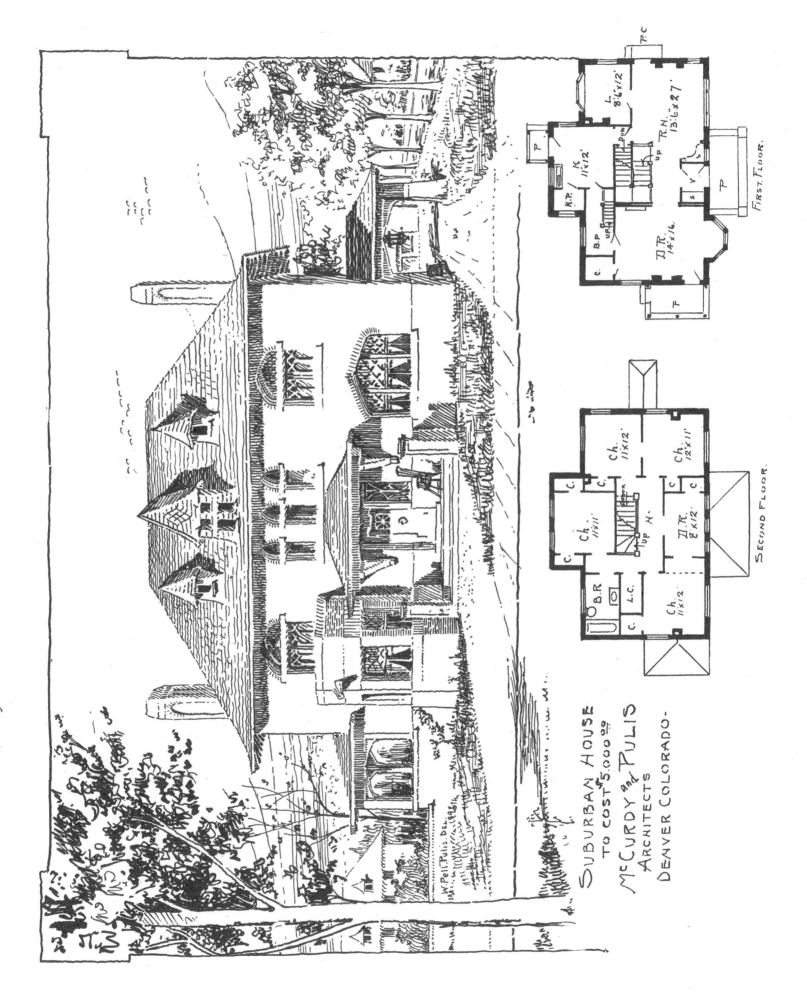

SUBURBAN HOUSE
TO COST $5,000.00

McCURDY and PULIS
ARCHITECTS
DENVER COLORADO.

First Floor.

Second Floor.

PLATES XXV., XXVI. AND XXVII.

THIS is a summer house, though its plan is fairly well adapted to year-round use, in case the feature of a hall living room is desired. This feature of the family assembly room, containing the main staircase, is getting more and more popular for houses of moderate size. Where there is also a back staircase this frank exposure of the main stairs is advantageous every way, both on score of looks and convenience.

The location of this house is on the crown of a ledge at Biddeford Pool, near the mouth of the Saco River. The stonework is of mossy stone, taken from old stone walls, which have been replaced by rustic fences. The stones are laid dry, pointed on the inside; no pointing, however, for two face piazza or terrace walls. Mortar washings destroy the moss on stonework. By laying the wall dry the moss is saved, and a more picturesque effect generally is got than with a mortar-jointed wall.

The external wood walls are shingled with cedar, left natural, and weathered a handsome silver gray. The trimmings are light buff, the blinds warm olive.

Internally the color scheme of living room and dining room is worth noting. The dining room has much the more woodwork, a dado three feet high and a timbered ceiling. The living room and staircase finish is according to the sectional drawing. The same wall paper is used for both rooms, a Renaissance pattern, ivory-white figure on a subdued moss-green field. The ivory-white of the paper is matched in the paint of the living room woodwork. The moss-green of the paper is matched in the stain of the dining room work, including the timbered ceiling. The combined effect of the two rooms is charmingly harmonious. Bits of tawny and russet and blue color are introduced in draperies, rugs and scarfs.

The chambers in second story have some sloping walls, though the large dormers make these rooms ample. The vertical walls, slopes and ceilings are papered with the same pattern wall paper, and the treatment is artistically successful. The cost of the house is $5,000, exclusive of wall papers and chandeliers.

Albert Winslow Cobb
Architect
Winthrop Highlands
Mass.

Plate XXV.

Suburban and Country Homes.

A HOUSE IN MAINE. — Albert Winslow Cobb, Architect.

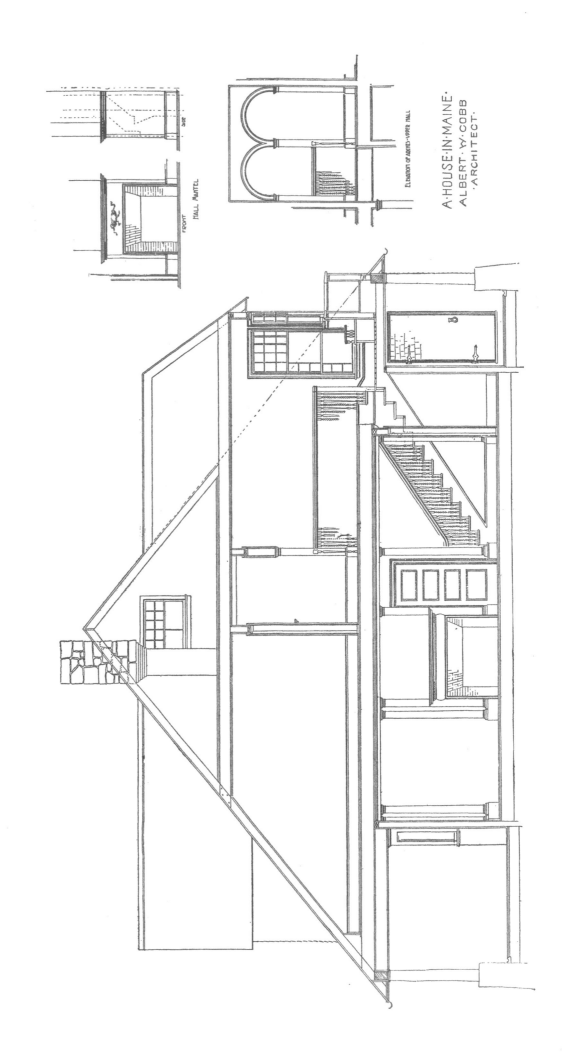

Plate XXVI.

Suburban and Country Homes.

A·HOUSE·IN·MAINE·
ALBERT· W· COBB
·ARCHITECT·

ELEVATION OF ARCHES~UPPER HALL

FRONT
SIDE
HALL MANTEL

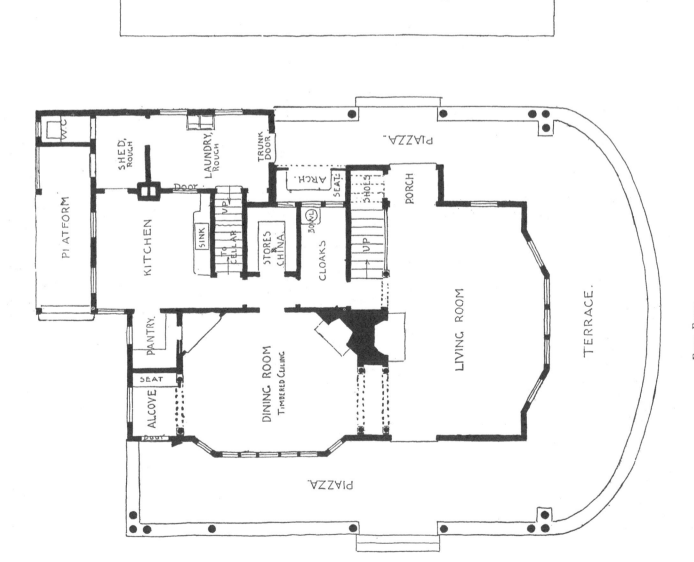

Plate XXVII.

Suburban and Country Homes.

SECOND FLOOR.

FIRST FLOOR.

PLATES XXVIII. AND XXIX.

THIS house was erected at Bensonhurst-by-the-Sea, N. Y. The interior is finished throughout in whitewood, designed in the Colonial style, in keeping with the exterior. The first and second stories have double floors, with heavy building paper between. The rooms are simply arranged, as shown in the plans, and a description is hardly necessary. The third floor contains three large rooms and trunk room. The cellar has cemented floor and plastered ceiling, and contains furnace, laundry and servants' water closet. The plumbing is of the best; all pipes and fixtures in bathroom are nickel-plated. Estimated cost, $8,500.

E. G. W. Dietrich
Architect
18 Broadway
New York

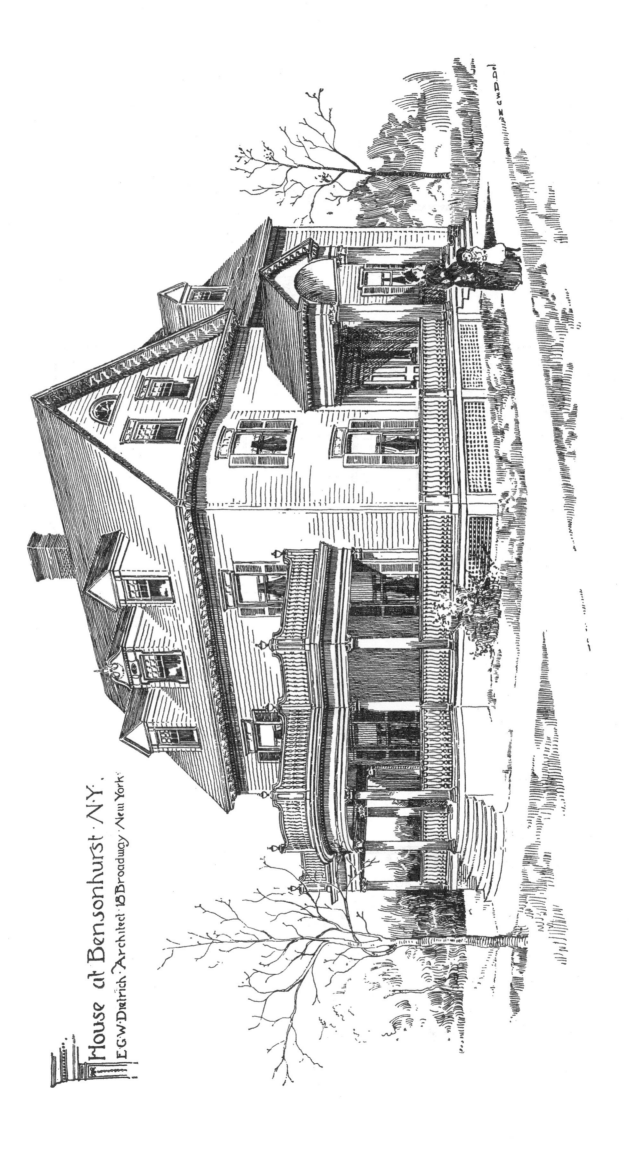

Plate XXVIII.

Suburban and Country Homes.

House at Bensonhurst · N·Y·

E·G·W·Dietrich Architect · 18 Broadway · New York ·

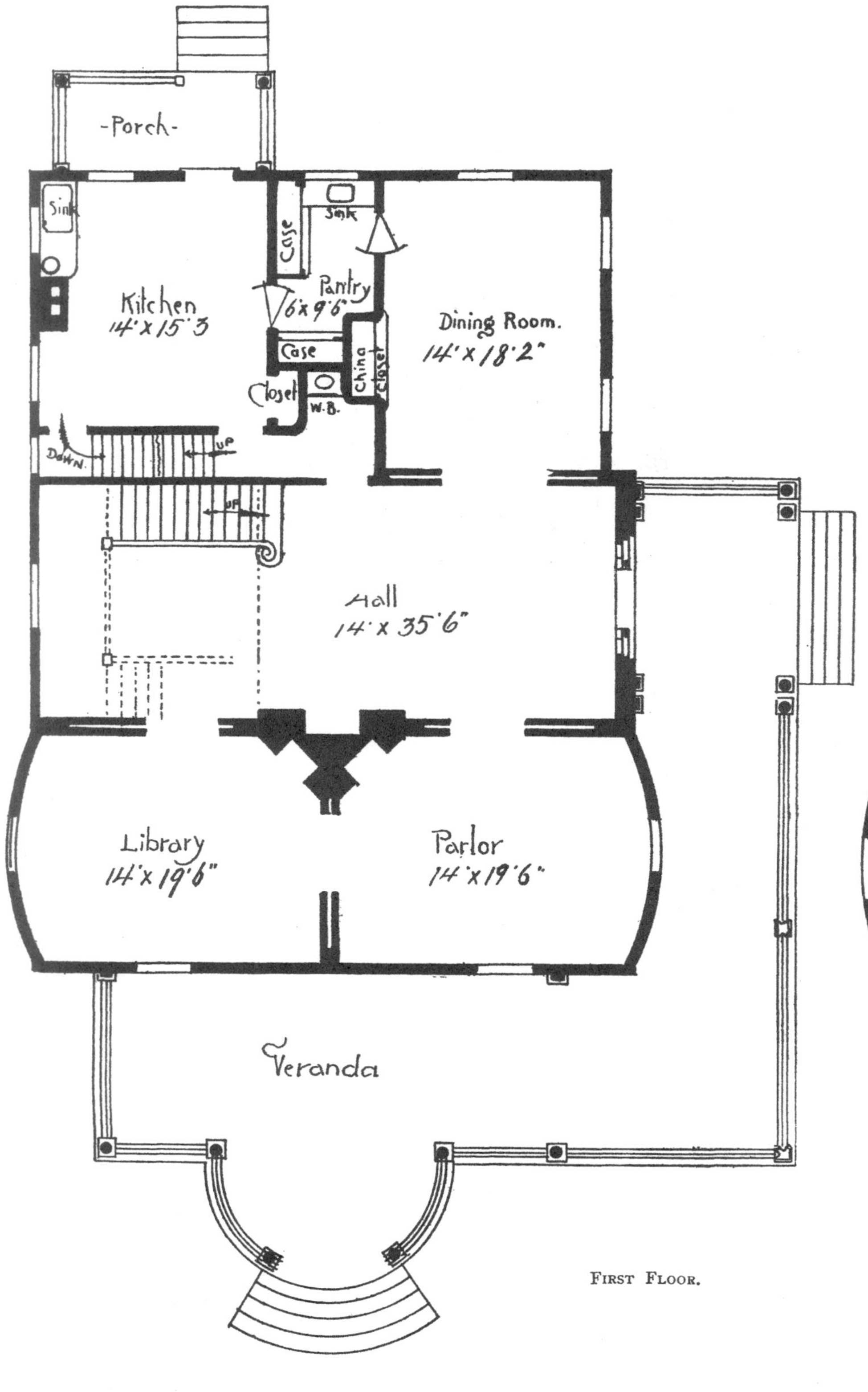

Plate XXIX.

Suburban and Country Homes.

Second Floor

Bed Room
14'x23'

Bath Room
6'x15'

Closet

Bed Room
12'x14'

Hall

Closet

Closet

Closet

Linen Closet

Hall

Nook

Seat

Closet

well

Up

Platform

Down

Bed Room
17'x20'

Bed Room
14'x17'6"

Balcony

SECOND FLOOR

First Floor

Porch

Kitchen
14'x15'3

Dining Room.
14'x18'2"

Pantry
6'x9'6"

China Closet

Case

W.B.

Closet

Hall
14'x35'6"

Up

Down

Parlor
14'x19'6"

Library
14'x19'6"

Veranda

FIRST FLOOR.

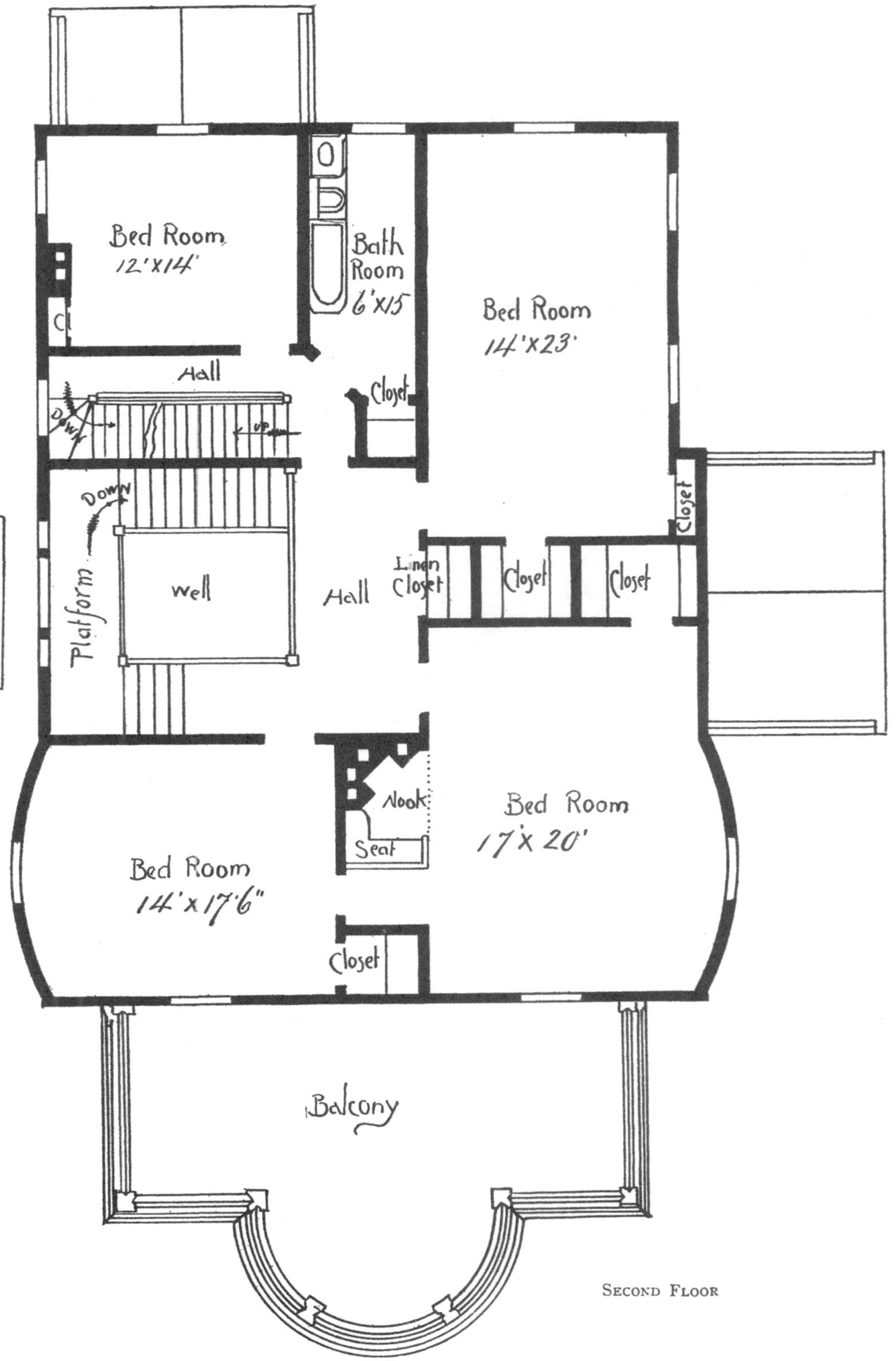

PLATES XXX. AND XXXI.

THIS house is arranged to contain on the first floor: Parlor, 12' 6"x18' 6"; library of circular form; reception hall, 12' 6"x12' 6"; dining room, 15' 6"x17' 6", and kitchen, 12' 6"x14' 6", with butler's pantry. The second floor has four large bedrooms and bath. The interior is finished in whitewood, stained or left natural. The exterior is covered with shingles, stained. Cost, about $4,000.

John Brower, Jr.
Architect
Riverside Drive and 109th St.
New York

·A·COZY·HOME·OF·MODERATE·COST·

John Brower Jr Arch't   Riverside Drive & 109 th St   New York City

Plate XXXI.

Suburban and Country Homes.

FRONT ELEVATION.

SECOND FLOOR PLAN.

SIDE ELEVATION.

FIRST FLOOR PLAN.

PLATES XXXII. AND XXXIII.

THIS house was built at Bensonhurst-by-the-Sea, N. Y., and overlooks Gravesend Bay, with Fort Hamilton and Staten Island in the distance. The first floor contains reception hall, parlor, den, dining room and kitchen, with butler's pantry, and a large porch both front and rear. The second floor has four bedrooms and bath. A dressing room connects with one of the front rooms, or could answer for both if desired. The interior trim is of whitewood, painted in some rooms and stained or left natural in others. The parlor is finished in ivory enamel paint. Cost, including plumbing and heating, $5,000.

E. G. W. Dietrich
Architect
18 Broadway
New York

Plate XXXII.

Suburban and Country Homes.

HOUSE AT.
BENSONHURST
N.Y.

ARCHITECT.
E.G.W.DIETRICH
NEW YORK.

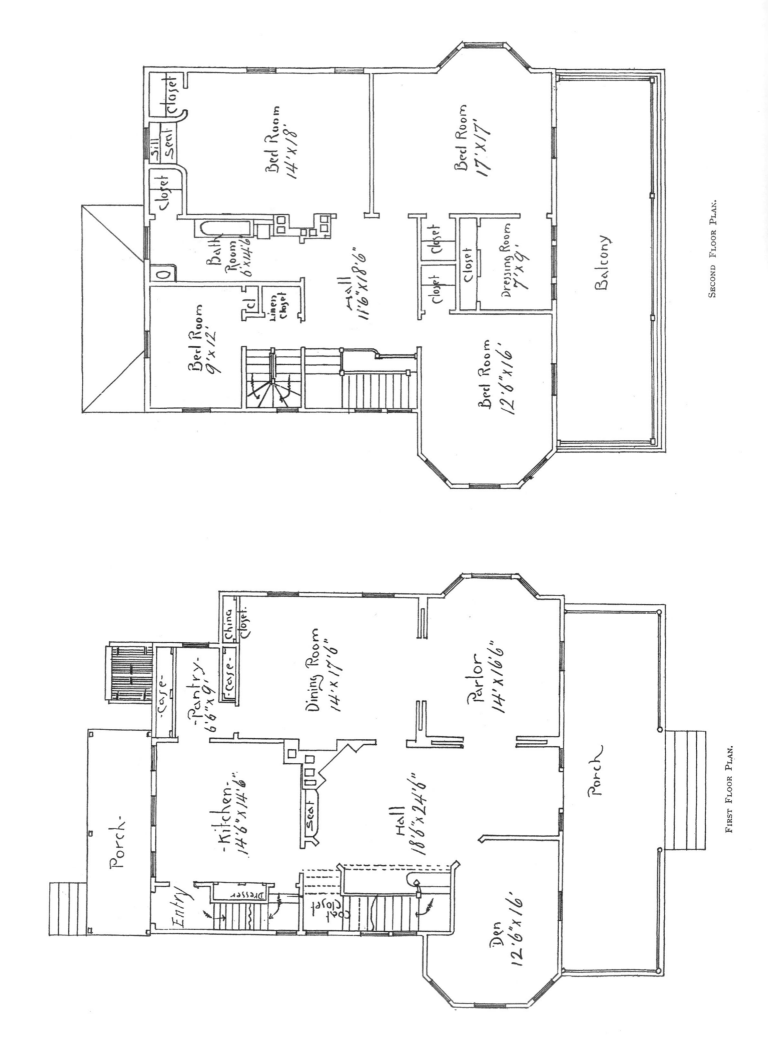

Suburban and Country Homes.

Plate XXXIII.

Second Floor Plan:

Closet

Sill Seat

Closet

Bed Room
14' x 18'

Bed Room
17' x 17'

Bath Room
6' x 14' 6"

Linen Closet

Hall
11' 6" x 18' 6"

Closet

Closet

Closet

Dressing Room
7' x 9'

Bed Room
9' x 12'

Bed Room
12' 6" x 16'

Balcony

SECOND FLOOR PLAN.

First Floor Plan:

Porch

Case

Pantry
6' 6" x 9'

Case

Case

China Closet

Kitchen
14' 6" x 14' 6"

Dining Room
14' x 17' 6"

Seat

Entry

Dresser

Coat Closet

Hall
18' 6" x 24' 6"

Parlor
14' x 16' 6"

Porch

Den
12' 6" x 16'

FIRST FLOOR PLAN.

PLATES XXXIV. AND XXXV.

A HOUSE now in course of erection and is planned to contain on the first floor reception hall, parlor, dining room and kitchen. The hall is finished in oak and has an open grate and cosy nook. The kitchen has range, sink, china closet and cold closet, and communicates with the dining room through the butler's pantry, which contains wash tray and shelving. The parlor is finished in white and gold and the dining room in oak. All woodwork is of a simple Colonial character. The second floor has four bedrooms and bath, together with a number of closets; all rooms on this floor are finished in pine, painted. Cost, including plumbing and furnace, $4,900.

A. L. C. Marsh
Architect
90 Nassau Street
New York

Plate XXXIV.

Suburban and Country Homes.

·REAR·VIEW·.

·PERSPECTIVE·

·A·L·C·MARSH· ARCHITECT·
·92·NASSAU·ST· NEW·YORK·

·A·C·MARSH· DEL· 1892·

Plate XXXV.

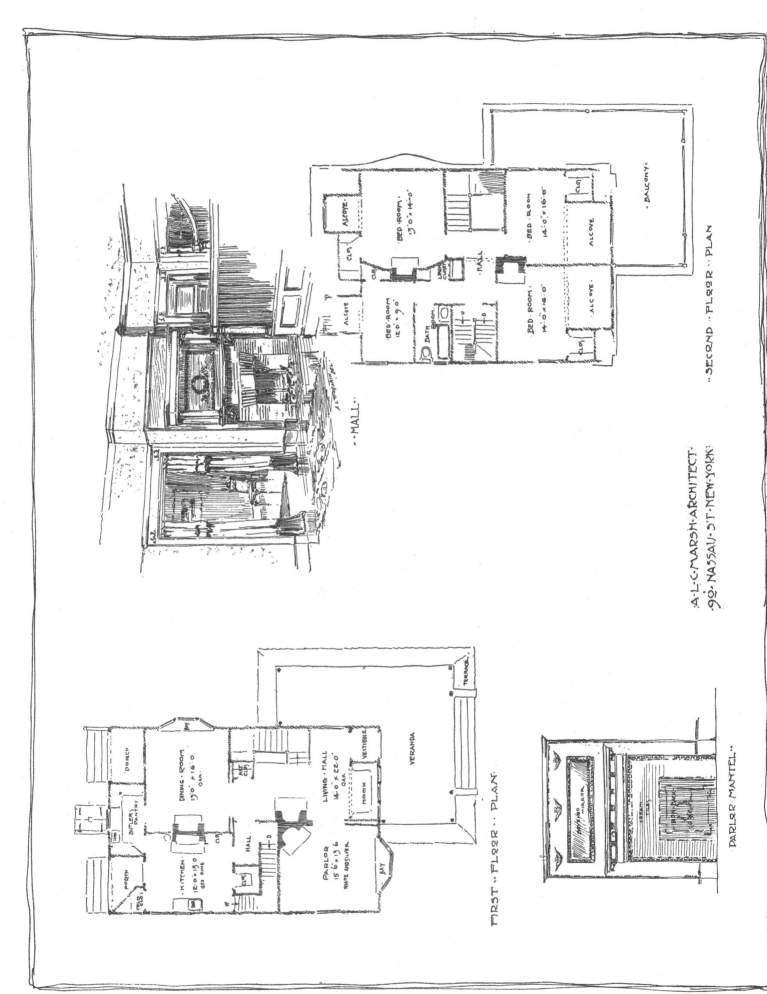

·A·L·C·MARSH·ARCHITECT·
·92· NASSAU· ST· NEW·YORK·

·SECOND ··FLOOR ·· PLAN·

·FIRST ··FLOOR ·· PLAN·

·PARLOR · MANTEL·

PLATES XXXVI. AND XXXVII.

THIS house has recently been erected at Nutley, N. J. The first floor contains library, parlor, dining room, kitchen and laundry. A large pantry fitted with wash tray and shelving separates the dining room and kitchen and serves as a passage. The second floor has three bedrooms, dressing room, bath and ample closets. Three rooms are finished in the attic. The interior is finished in whitewood and has double floors. The walls and ceilings are plastered and tinted in kalsomine. The exterior is of clapboards and roof of cypress shingles. Cost, including plumbing and furnace, $4,500.

E. R. Tilton
Architect
21 State Street
New York

Plate XXXVI.

Suburban and Country Homes.

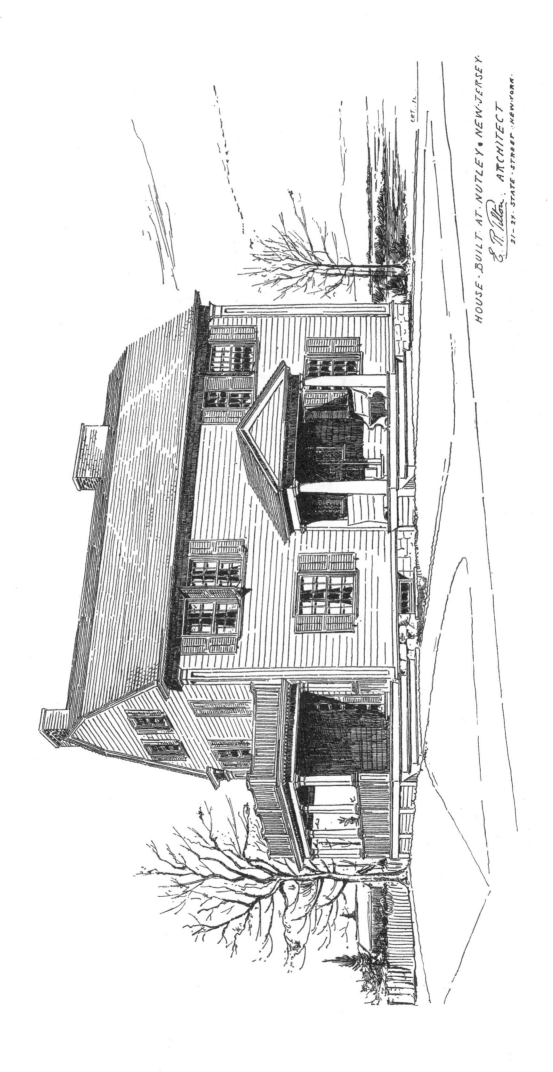

HOUSE · BUILT · AT · NUTLEY ● NEW · JERSEY.

E. T. Allen · ARCHITECT

21 – 23 · STATE · STREET · NEW · YORK.

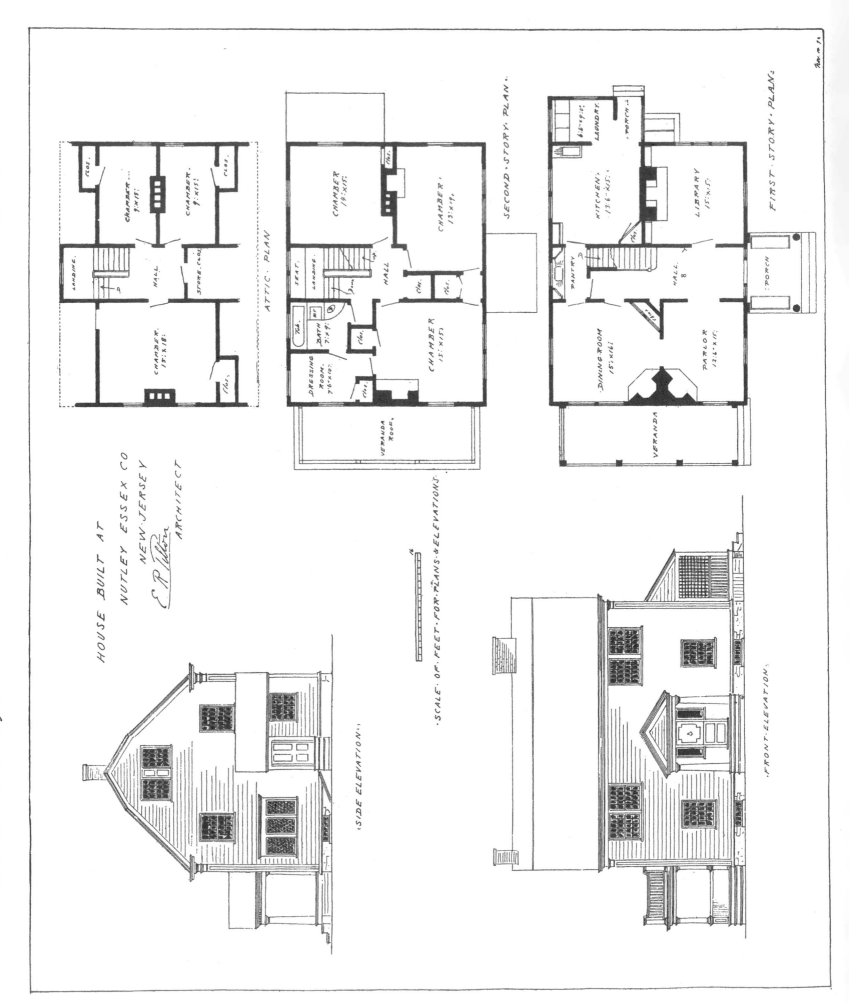

Plate XXXVII.

Suburban and Country Homes.

CHAMBER.
9'×15'.

CHAMBER.
9'×15'.

CLOS.

CLOS.

LANDING.

HALL

STORE CLOS.

CHAMBER.
15'×18'.

CLOS.

·ATTIC·PLAN·

CHAMBER
18'×15'

CHAMBER
15'×19'

SEAT.

LANDING

HALL

CLO.

CLO.

DRESSING
ROOM.
7'6"×10'

BATH
7'×9'.

CLO.

CLO.

CHAMBER
15'×15'.

CLO.

VERANDA
ROOF.

·SECOND·STORY·PLAN·

KITCHEN.
13'6"×15'.

LAUNDRY.
6'9"×9'6".

PORCH.

PANTRY

CLO.

LIBRARY
15'×15'.

HALL
8'

CLO.

DINING·ROOM
15'×16½'.

PARLOR
12'6"×15'.

VERANDA

PORCH.

·FIRST·STORY·PLAN·

HOUSE BUILT AT
NUTLEY ESSEX CO
NEW·JERSEY
E. P. Pilton
ARCHITECT

·SCALE·OF·FEET·FOR·PLANS·&·ELEVATIONS·

·SIDE·ELEVATION·

·FRONT·ELEVATION·

PLATE XXXVIII.

THIS house was recently built at Benson-hurst-by-the-Sea, N. Y., and presents a neat and most homelike appearance. The exterior is covered with clap-boards, painted yellow, with white trimmings. The roof is of shingles stained a dark green. The interior is well planned and space used to the best advantage. The simple Colonial nature. Cost, including plumbing and heating, $5,200.

First Floor.

Second Floor.

E. G. W. Dietrich
Architect
18 Broadway
New York

Suburban and Country Homes.

Plate XXXVIII.

HOUSE ~ BENSON-
HURST ... N.Y ... E. G. W. DI-
ETRICH ... 18 BROADWAY ...
NEW YORK. ARCH'T

PLATES XXXIX. AND XL.

WE here present a house situated at Yonkers, N. Y. The first floor is composed of a reception hall, parlor, study, dining room and kitchen, a large piazza extending across the front and part of the side. The kitchen is fitted with stationary range, hot water boiler, sink and tubs—a large closet and a butler's pantry connecting with the dining room. This pantry is fitted with sink and wash trays. The second floor has four bedrooms and bathroom. The attic contains three bedrooms and has ample room for storage purposes. The interior trim is of hardwood. Plumbing of good quality. The exterior is covered with shingles, stained. Cost, about $5,000.

Creighton Withers
Architect
21 State Street
New York

Plate XXXIX.

Suburban and Country Homes.

COTTAGE
BUILT AT
YONKERS·N·Y
CREIGHTON·WITHERS·
ARCHITECT·NEW·YORK·CITY

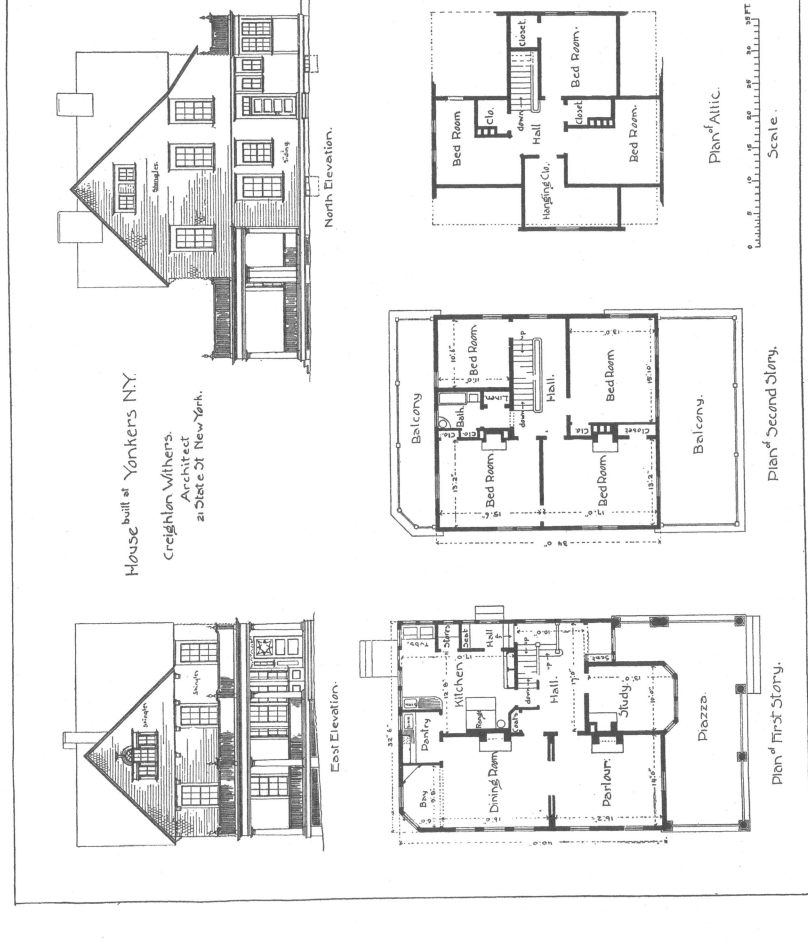

Plate XL.

Suburban and Country Homes.

House built at Yonkers N.Y.

Creighton Withers.
Architect
21 State St New York.

North Elevation.

East Elevation.

Plan of Attic.

Scale.

Plan of Second Story.

Plan of First Story.

PLATES XLI. AND XLII.

OUR illustrations in these plates represent a cottage of moderate cost, approximately $5,000, according to the locality and the quality and style of materials used in its construction. The plan is conveniently arranged and embraces several attractive features. The first story consists of reception hall, parlor, dining room, kitchen and pantry. The second story contains four chambers and bath, while three or four rooms could be finished in the attic, according to the requirements of the owner. The exterior indicates shingles, with a little stone work introduced. The color scheme could be natural shingles with white trimmings, or a stained effect with dark finish for a contrast.

F. W. Beall.
Architect.
318 Broadway
New York

Suburban and Country Homes.

Plate XLI.

Suggestions For A Cottage

F.W. Beall Arch't.
518. B'way. N.Y.

Plate XLII.

Suburban and Country Homes.

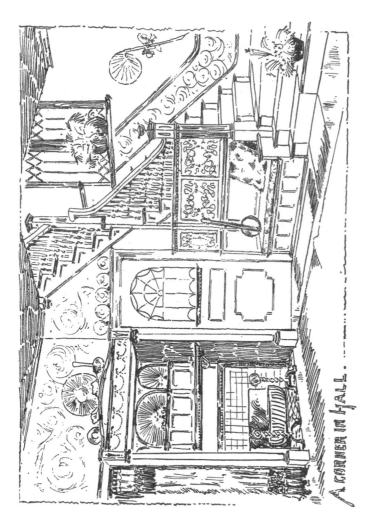

A CORNER IN HALL.

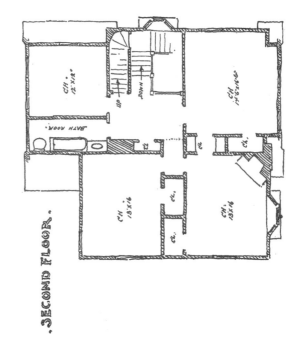

SECOND FLOOR.

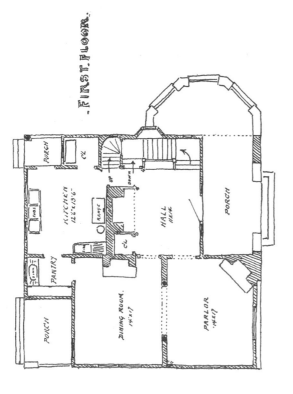

FIRST FLOOR.

A CORNER IN DINING ROOM.

PLATES XLIII. AND XLIV.

IN these illustrations is given a house suitable for a thirty-foot lot, and consists of reception hall, parlor, dining room, kitchen and butler's pantry. The second floor contains three bedrooms and bath, with ample closets. The exterior to height of second floor is covered with clapboards and the remainder of shingles. The roof is also shingled. The interior is finished in both hard and whitewood, the hall being in oak, parlor in white and gold, and dining room in cherry. The cost will vary between $3,000 and $4,000, according to locality.

John Brower, Jr.
Architect
Riverside Drive and 109th St.
New York

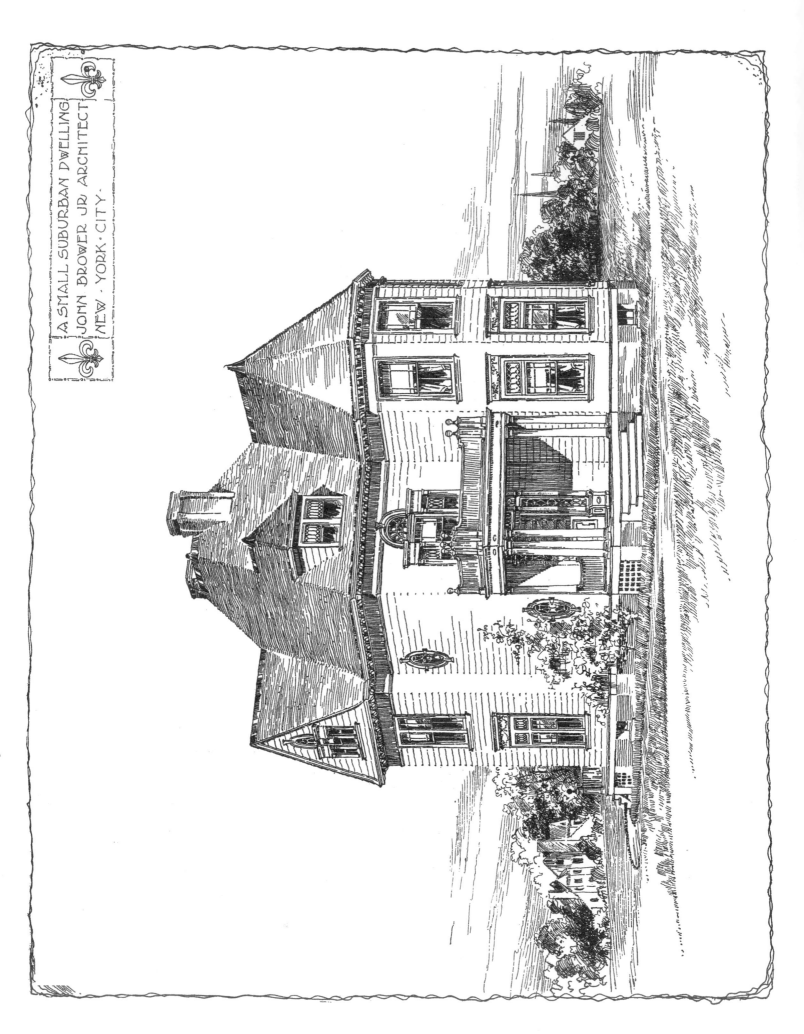

Suburban and Country Homes.

Plate XLIII.

A SMALL SUBURBAN DWELLING
JOHN BROWER JR ARCHITECT
NEW · YORK · CITY ·

Plate XLIV.

Suburban and Country Homes.

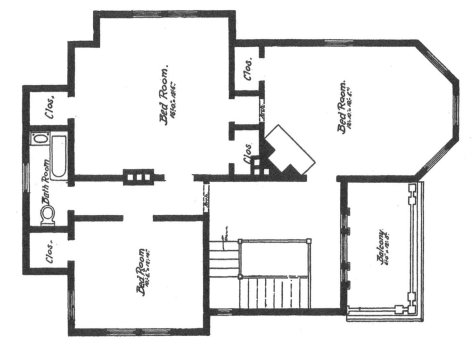

Second Floor Plan.

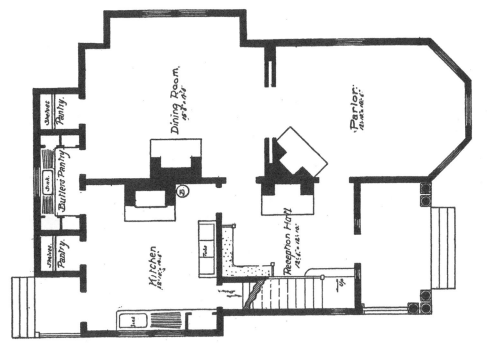

First Floor Plan—